# look
## before you
# leap

AN ADVICE AND RIGHTS
GUIDE FOR
CHOREOGRAPHERS

## Ann Whitley

This is not a book about how to
choreograph. It is a practical
guide to the negotiation,
preparation, organisation and
continuing care of choreographic
work. It is intended as a useful
source of reference for
choreographers, assistant
choreographers, managers,
choreologists, dance teachers,
administrators, animateurs,
movement specialists, composers,
designers, technicians, and all
those who collaborate with
choreographers.

# Dance UK

**Look Before You Leap: An Advice and Rights Guide for Choreographers** *by Ann Whitley*

Published by:
*Dance UK*
*23 Crisp Road*
*London W6 9RL*

October 1995

Edited by: Andrea Phillips
Designed by: Baskerville 0181 870 4980
Printed by: Instant Print West One

ISBN: 0-9515631-2-2

Dance UK is funded by the Arts Council of England.

*This book has been published with the generous financial support of the Equity Trust Fund, the Paul Hamlyn Foundation and Gillian Lynne.*

# Dance UK
## A voice for dance

Professional dancers and dance companies need co-ordinated representation nationally and internationally and a forum for debate. Dance UK was formed in 1982 in a response to a demand from many parts of the profession to find such a united voice.

Dance UK campaigns on behalf of the profession, organises seminars, meetings and conferences which bring together professionals and experts in national and international dance, liaises with other art forms and allied professions and offers services, information and advice to its members. Dance UK's membership comprises dance companies, venues, organisations, individual dance artists, administrators, technicians, teachers and members of the audience.

### Vision into practice

Dance UK has spent some years developing a relationship between medical and dance experts concerned with dancers' health and welfare. Through the organisation of international conferences—**The Healthier Dancer** (1990) and **Training Tomorrow's Professional Dancers** (1993), Dance UK has developed the opportunities for these experts to communicate with the wider dance profession. Similarly, Dance UK has supported this work through the setting up of a **Medical Register** of orthodox and complementary practitioners with special interest and knowledge of dance injuries; the publication of an **Information Sheet Series** on health and other topics; the publication of **A Dancer's Charter**; and the organisation of a series of 'Roadshows' throughout the country offering professional dancers the opportunity to learn at first hand from health and welfare experts.

In 1992 Dr Peter Brinson gave this work fresh impetus by donating the money from his Digital Dance Premier Award to commission an enquiry and research into the issues of dancers' health and injuries. His vision on how to address this critical area began to work in partnership with Dance UK's developing interest and knowledge of the field. The chief result is the Healthier Dancer Programme Report.

Dance UK has also involved itself in the issue of provision for dance through its facilitation of the dance profession's debate and planning of a national dance house.

Inspired by those with vision and expertise, Dance UK continues to respond in practical ways. This publication, **Look Before You Leap: An Advice and Rights Guide for Choreographers,** is a further example of Dance UK's aim to provide practical guidance and advice to the profession, in this case, principally choreographers. Dance UK is very grateful to all those who contributed to this project and would like to thank colleagues at Equity and the British Association of Choreographers for their help and support in its preparation. We hope that all will regard this publication as an indication of our commitment to support choreographers, present and future, and their provision of the life blood of our art form.

# Dance UK resources

Some of the resources currently available from Dance UK are:

## Dance UK News
A quarterly magazine offering news, views and information
£1 (free to members)

## A Handbook for Dance Floors
by Mark Foley
£10 (£7.50 to members)

## Information Sheet Series
Covering selected topics including avoiding injury, nutrition, tax, insurance and first aid (free to members)

## A Dancer's Charter
Advice on rights, health and welfare (free to members)

## Dance healthcare posters
(free to members)

# For information on membership contact:

Dance UK
23 Crisp Road
London W6 9RL
Telephone: +44 (0) 181 741 1932
Facsimile:  +44 (0) 181 748 0186
e-mail:      danceuk@gn.abc.org

to Bob, Dick and Stuart

who said something should
be done...

## Special thanks to

Jane Attenborough, *Director, Dance UK;* Andrea Phillips, *editor;* Imogen Claire, *choreographer, Chair of Equity's Choreographers' Committee and councillor;* Stuart Hopps, *choreographer, Chair of the British Association of Choreographers;* Dick Matchett, *freelance dance administrator;* John Robinson, *Equity Opera, Ballet and Overseas Theatre Organiser;* Sir Peter Wright, *Director Laureate, Birmingham Royal Ballet;* and Dance UK, who facilitated the research and commissioned the publication of this book.

## Thanks to

Avril Anderson, *composer and lecturer in music;* Lea Anderson, *choreographer, The Cholmondeleys and The Featherstonehaughs;* Nadine Baylis, *theatre designer;* Val Bourne, *Director, Dance Umbrella;* Theresa Buckland, *Dance Anthropologist, University of Surrey;* Simon Byford, *freelance production manager;* Roy Campbell-Moore, *Artistic Director, Diversions;* Gill Clarke, *choreographer, performer and teacher;* Michael Corder, *freelance choreographer;* Ken Cordingley, *Musicians' Union;* Fiona Dick, *arts advisor;* Fergus Early, *Artistic Director, Green Candle Dance Company;* Education Welfare Service, City of Westminster; Eleanor Fazan, *freelance choreographer;* Kate Flatt, *freelance choreographer;* Mark Foley, *architect, Burrell Foley Fischer;* Craig Givens, *designer;* Paul Goddard, *Arts Development Officer, Dartington Arts;* Noël Goodwin, *freelance writer and critic;* Adrian Grater, *Technical Director, the Benesh Institute;* Richard Haigh, *Performing Arts;* Michael Holmes, *freelance choreographer;* Madeline Hutchins, *freelance arts management consultant and trainer;* Robert Israel, *Gordon and Company Insurance Brokers;* Linda Jasper, *Chair, Community Dance and Mime Foundation;* Jean Johnson-Jones, *Director, Labanotation Institute;* Robert Jude, *freelance video consultant, Manager, Royal Ballet Video Archive;* Emma Kerr, *Boosey and Hawkes Music Publishers;* Rosemary Lee, *choreographer;* Bob Lockyer, *producer, BBC Television;* Gillian Lynne, *choreographer;* Judy Mackerras, *Surtitles Co-ordinator, Royal Opera House;* Vernon Mound, *freelance opera director;* Anne Murray, *dance programmes, BBC Television;* MJ O'Shaughnessy; Caroline Pope, *freelance choreographer;* Jane Pritchard, *Archivist, Rambert Dance Company and English National Ballet;* Debby Pulford, *Office Manager, Dance UK;* Derek Purnell, *Administrative Director, Birmingham Royal Ballet;* Quinny Sacks, *freelance choreographer;* Denni Sayers, *freelance choreographer;* Val Schöne, *Children's Co-ordinator, Royal Opera House;* Prudence Skene, *arts consultant and Chair of Arts Council of England's Dance Panel;* Katy Spicer, *General Manager, Green Candle Dance Company;* Gus Stewart, *freelance lighting designer;* Jeremy Sutcliffe, *Head of Staff Directors, Royal Opera House;* David Sutton-Anderson, *composer, conductor and lecturer in music;* Jane Turner, *choreographer, teacher, Artistic Director, Turning Worlds;* Elaine Tyler-Hall, *freelance choreologist;* Anthony van Laast, *freelance choreographer;* David Williams, *Administration and Personnel Manager, English National Ballet;* Ginnie Wollaston, *Education and Development Officer, Shobana Jeyasingh Dance Company.*

Ann Whitley studied at the Royal Ballet School and the Benesh Institute of Choreology. She was Rambert Dance Company's first choreologist and director of its educational unit. In addition to her work with dance, she has since 1977 pioneered the use of Benesh notation in opera and musical theatre productions, notating and re-staging choreography for dancers, singers and actors both nationally and internationally. She has worked with many choreographers and companies and undertaken a variety of administrative and teaching assignments in the dance world. She is a fellow of the Benesh Institute.

# Foreword

*by Sir Peter Wright, Director Laureate,*
*Birmingham Royal Ballet*

At last a book that will help both new and experienced choreographers when tackling the tricky problems encountered in the pursuit of choreographic production and negotiation.

For a long time choreographers have been struggling for better facilities and contractual conditions for their vital creative work, which embraces a wide range of dance techniques, cultures, participants and forms of presentation. What a joy it now is to have this reference book written by such a professional. It refers to all the different stages of choreography, from the initial commission to the first performance and throughout the life of the created work. It describes the practical needs of the choreographer for public dance performances and aspects of educational work, for operas, musicals, pantomime, plays, television and film, whether in conventional or unusual locations.

The book is clearly set out, brilliantly researched, and is a 'must' for all those involved in the presentation of choreographic works including stage, costume and lighting designers, composers, producers and agents. No stone is left unturned as we are alerted to problems and pitfalls, from copyright to rehearsal conditions, contracts to health insurance, sound reproduction to union regulations, whether in large opera houses or small amateur theatres. Not only are problems exposed but ways and means to solve them are carefully explained.

I shall now keep this vital and comprehensive reference book with me at all times, and am hugely grateful to Ann Whitley and Dance UK for helping to make the way ahead clearer and better for choreographers everywhere.

All artists learn by trial and error, and more often than not, in the public view. Choreographers are no exception. We are up there on trial with our work and this can be daunting, particularly at the beginning.

How I wish **Look Before You Leap** had existed when I first began to choreograph in the mid-1950s—the days when every producer approached you with 'of course, we didn't budget for a choreographer...'

This is a book that treats choreography with the respect it deserves, and by its comprehensive and practical advice will do much to smooth the path for choreographers and affirm their art as an important branch of the performing arts.

**Eleanor Fazan, choreographer**

# CONTENTS

HOW TO USE THIS GUIDE ................................................................... xii
INTRODUCTION ............................................................................. xiii
CONTENTS CHECKLIST ....................................................................xiv

**PART ONE**
Contract ........................................................................................ 3
Money.......................................................................................... 11
Agents and managers .................................................................19
Equity .......................................................................................... 24

**PART TWO**
Working as a choreographer ........................................................31

**PART THREE**
Working as a choreographer in opera and musical theatre ...................53
Working as a choreographer for a play .............................................62
Working as a choreographer for a film ..............................................67
Working as a choreographer for an advertising commercial ...................74
Working as a choreographer for television: three examples ...................79
Working as a choreographer with schools and youth organisations ......... 85
Working as a choreographer in the community .................................... 92
Working as a choreographer for a specific site or occasion: organisation ......... 96
Working abroad ........................................................................... 103

**PART FOUR**
Assistants, notators and staff producers ......................................... 111
Music ........................................................................................ 120
Set and costume design ...............................................................130
Lighting design ...........................................................................136
Videotapes ................................................................................139

**PART FIVE**
Insurance ...................................................................................145
Copyright ...................................................................................151
Health and safety ........................................................................156
Child performance regulations ...................................................... 162

**FURTHER INFORMATION**
Useful Addresses .............................................................. Booklet
Useful Publications............................................................ Booklet
Sample Equity Contracts .................................................... Booklet

Some people may read **Look Before You Leap** from beginning to end while others will look for specific advice immediately. The order of the chapters is not intended to dictate an order of priority for your reading. In practice, many aspects of preparation and discussion about choreographic work are likely to develop simultaneously and the individual approach of both choreographer and management may bring its own emphasis and order of importance to certain topics.

The guide is divided into five parts. In Part Two, the chapter **Working as a choreographer**, although written with a slight bias towards working in a dance company, is intended as a 'foundation' chapter for work in many related fields. The chapters which follow in Part Three, covering work in plays, opera, film, television, education and so on, focus on additional information, but do not repeat advice already contained in **Working as a choreographer.**

The *See also* references which appear throughout the text are intended to divert your attention to subjects which may have additional or unexpected relevance to your field of practice. If a paragraph does not seem to apply to your work, check any *See also* notes before moving on, since these might divert you to another chapter or sub-section where there is more applicable advice.

You will find addresses and publications referred to within the chapters listed in the booklet enclosed, which has been designed separately so that it can be updated in the future.

There are several checklists in this guide, the most extensive of which is the **Contents Checklist** on pages xiv–xvii which is designed to be photocopied.

*Note: In this publication, the terms 'United Kingdom' and 'UK' refer to England, Wales, Scotland and Northern Ireland.*

For many years I have been involved in international efforts to improve conditions of employment for movement notators. The more diverse my work has become, the more convinced I am that if my place within a production team is to be clearly recognised, my work more effective, and my contracts more appropriate, improvements are also needed to conditions of engagement for the choreographers with whom I work. My tendency is to surround myself with checklists. I wondered whether these might be developed for use by other dance professionals. My response was *A Handbook for Choreography*, first published by Dance UK in 1989.

As with many guide books, some information soon needs revision and extension. This publication attempts to reach a broader readership of choreographers and their assistants working nationally and internationally.

**Look Before You Leap** draws attention to important contractual and practical matters which might be overlooked by a choreographer moving into a new field of work. It offers informal advice about the negotiation, preparation and care of choreographic work, large or small-scale. As a source of reference for those entering the profession and those with many years' experience, the guide recognises distinct choreographic processes and respects differences in the approach and resources of managements.

The new publication contains advice on specific problems of perennial concern to choreographers, performers and administrators, but does not claim to focus comprehensively on the jobs of **all** those who collaborate in the production process. **Look Before You Leap** aims to provide a tool which is useful to a wide range of choreographers irrespective of their specialism or chosen dance style or form. However, the culture and traditions of non-Western dance forms may require additional considerations not covered in this edition.

Professional advice on certain subjects proved interestingly contradictory. Sidestepping the lack of consensus, I have used self-addressed questions which raise important issues without providing definitive answers. To the challenge that many of the subjects addressed in the book 'shouldn't be the responsibility of the choreographer', I would answer that people from many branches of the dance profession endorse my view that it is an advantage to be informed about all matters which affect one's work. Hence, the rather frequent use of the exhortations 'check' and 'ask'.

**Look Before You Leap** does not separately address the subject of touring, although many references alert the reader to its implications. Neither does it provide administrative advice about setting up a company from scratch. When references are made to work abroad, more refer to Europe than to other continents.

It is Dance UK's and my wish that this book complements the work of the Equity Choreographers' Committee to widen the range of Equity contracts, and that it supports the role of the British Association of Choreographers. I hope that the guide will help to raise the profile of choreographers and bring greater respect to the nature of their work within the arts. Dance UK would welcome any comments or suggestions you have for future editions.

**Ann Whitley**
October 1995

# CONTENTS CHECKLIST

## PART ONE

### Contract
1. The offer
2. What is a contract?
3. What is a schedule?
4. Checking your contract
5. Revivals, transfers and adaptations
6. If things go wrong
7. Negotiations

### Money
1. Choreographic fee—payment
2. Royalties and residuals
3. Choreographic fee—deductions
4. Expenses:
   *Travel*
   *Accommodation*
   *Subsistence*
   *Incidental*
5. Employment status
6. National Insurance contributions
7. Accountants
8. Unpaid work
9. Union membership

### Agents and managers
1. What is an agent or manager?
2. How to find an agent or manager
3. The initial meeting
4. What an agent-manager may or may not do
5. What an agent-manager expects from you
6. Changing agent-managers
7. Other management and production services

### Equity
1. Equity/TMA Agreement
2. Equity/SOLT Agreement
3. Contract details
4. Equity services
5. Choreographers' Register
6. Choreographers' Committee

## PART TWO

### Working as a choreographer
1. The choreography:
   *Title*
   *Length*
   *Full evening works and mixed programmes*
   *Other movement specialists*
   *First and future performances*
2. Rehearsals:
   *Time to create the work*
   *Schedules*
   *Clashing engagements*
   *Facilities—checklist*
   *Props*
   *Personal equipment*
3. Pre- and post- production meetings
4. Casting:
   *Adults*
   *Children*
   *Guest artists*
   *Availability of performers*
   *Animals and birds*
5. Audition procedure
6. Travel arrangements
7. Accommodation arrangements
8. Administrative tasks:
   *Personal details*
   *Company information*
   *A seat for the first performance*
   *Security pass*
9. Publicity
10. Programme credits:
    *Choreographer and choreography*
    *Cast and other contributors*
    *Sponsor and funding body*
    *Checklist*
11. Making a complaint
12. Transfers: consultation with the production team

**PART THREE**

**Working as a choreographer in opera and musical theatre**
1. What are you contracted to undertake?
2. Other choreographers or movement specialists
3. The creative hierarchy
4. Dates and times
5. Rehearsal sessions
6. Non-availability of performers
7. Printed rehearsal schedules
8. Company personnel lists
9. Cast lists
10. Programme credit
11. Actors, singers and 'non-dancers'
12. Microphones
13. Surtitles
14. Pre-performance warm-up or rehearsal
15. Post-production care

**Working as a choreographer for a play**
1. What are you contracted to undertake?
2. Your contract
3. Royalties
4. Rehearsals
5. Rehearsal assistants and dance captains
6. Re-casting and touring

**Working as a choreographer for a film**
1. Choice of choreographer
2. Discussions with the director
3. Negotiation, contract and fee
4. Casting and auditions
5. Working with the cast
6. Preparation
7. The choreographic process
8. Design
9. Music

**Working as a choreographer for an advertising commercial**
1. The production company, the client, the agency
2. First contact with the choreographer
3. The contract
4. Preparation
5. The production team
6. Performers, auditions, assistants and rehearsals
7. Shooting/filming

**Working as a choreographer for television: three examples**
1. Recording an extract of an existing choreographic work
2. Recording the whole of an existing choreographic work
3. Choreographic commissions for television
4. General notes
5. Editing
6. Contracts

**Working as a choreographer with schools and youth organisations**
1. What sort of choreographic work is expected?
2. Your contract or formal agreement
3. Future use of the choreography
4. Co-operation of parents, school or community staff
5. Double casting and understudies
6. Attendance at rehearsals or workshops
7. People with special needs
8. Facilities, supervision and assistance
9. Costume
10. Final or stage rehearsal
11. Pre-performance warm-up or rehearsal

# CONTENTS CHECKLIST

## Working as a choreographer in the community
1. Who do you work with?
2. How is the work done?
3. Is a performance appropriate?
4. Fees, contracts and cancellations
5. Insurance
6. Production costs
7. How to get experience

## Working as a choreographer for a specific site or occasion: organisation
1. Personnel
2. Insurance
3. Licensing
4. Administrator
5. Budget
6. Technical or production manager
7. Rehearsal and performance site
8. Sound engineer
9. Lighting requirements
10. Audience
11. Publicity
12. First aid
13. Emergency services
14. Get-in and get-out

## Working abroad
1. Checking your contract
2. Rehearsals and performers
3. Advice from Equity
4. Insurance
5. Passport
6. Visas and work permits
7. Health advice
8. Translator
9. Public holidays and industrial disputes
10. Consular advice
11. Before you go

# PART FOUR

## Assistants, notators and staff producers

### REHEARSAL ASSISTANTS
1. In the professional theatre (dance, opera and plays)
2. With children in theatre and education

### NOTATORS
1. The choreographic score
2. Ownership, security and use

### STAFF PRODUCERS
1. Preparation
2. Rehearsals
3. Performances
4. Revivals
5. Relationship with choreographer

## Music
1. The use of live and recorded music in public
2. Commissioned music
3. Working with conductors or musical directors
4. Scores and tapes
5. Rehearsal musicians
6. Programme and publicity credits for music
7. Learning more about music
8. The Musicians' Union

## Set and costume design
1. Discussions with the designer
2. The model
3. Costume considerations
4. Items for rehearsal—checklist
5. Floor surfaces
6. Footwear

**PART FIVE**

### Lighting design
1. What do you need?
2. The lighting session
3. Touring

### Videotapes
1. Making
2. Labelling
3. Copying
4. Storing
5. Travelling by air
6. Format

### Insurance
1. Insurance broker
2. The choreographer as employer
3. The choreographer as freelance artist

### Copyright
1. What is copyright?
2. Legislation
3. What works can have copyright protection?
4. Who owns copyright?
5. What action is needed to give copyright protection?
6. Periods of copyright protection and public domain
7. Permitted acts
8. Assignment and licence of copyright
9. International arrangements
10. Remedies for infringement of copyright
11. Moral rights
12. Collaborations
13. Further use
14. Using other people's copyright works

### Health and safety
1. First steps
2. First aid
3. AIDS/HIV prevention
4. Fire precautions
5. Fireproofing
6. During rehearsals
7. Special effects or equipment
8. Performance and backstage areas

### Child performance regulations
1. Summary of regulations
2. Examples of exceptions
3. General notes
4. Working abroad

PART 1

# PART 1

Contract

Money

Agents and Managers

Equity

# Contract

This chapter aims to provide an approach to contractual negotiations between you and a commissioning company or individual. The information contained here may be of particular value to choreographers entering the profession, and to those moving from the comparative shelter of a parent organisation with expert management into a new field of choreographic work (which may or may not be supported by the services of an agent or manager). The first part of this chapter outlines an ideal approach to contracts. Later, some aspects of 'normal practice' are considered.

1. The offer

2. What is a contract?

3. What is a schedule?

4. Checking your contract

5. Revivals, transfers and adaptations

6. If things go wrong

7. Negotiations

When considering work, whether on a large commercial production in the West End of London, or an event with a much smaller budget for amateur performers commissioned by a regional dance agency, always make sure you receive a contract or letter of agreement. Although verbal contracts are binding, they are an inadequate basis for business dealings. Remember that a management may seek to enforce a verbal agreement against you. **Always try to confirm arrangements in writing, including dates, in order to secure evidence, ensure clarity and prevent misunderstandings in the future. Get them in writing, even where arrangements are relatively small-scale or 'between friends'.**

## 1. The offer

Always try to distinguish between an offer and a preliminary check on your availability or other type of enquiry. Ask if you are not clear. Ask for any firm offer to be made in writing and state that if you wish to accept the offer you will do so in writing.

In any discussions make clear your availability and any of your professional or practical priorities. Reserve the right to study an offer and any special stipulations before any agreement is reached. In personal or telephone discussions, make dated notes of the points covered and any matters which will require more consideration.

Check that you have a common understanding at each stage and be wary of persistent vagueness, silence or long gaps between communications. **Make no assumptions.**

## 2. What is a contract?

A contract is a legally-binding agreement between two or more parties. It describes terms, conditions and undertakings applicable to each party—the management or commissioning company and you, 'The Choreographer'. You are likely to encounter various forms of contract or letter of agreement in addition to those negotiated by Equity.

There is no standard Equity agreement for choreographers working in either ballet or opera at present.

*See also:* **Equity** (page 24)

The wording, order and number of clauses in a contract will vary depending on the commissioning company or management and the nature and scale of the engagement. A standard contract may only cover a limited number of subjects relevant to the creation of a choreographic work. Examples of these are:

✦ the nature of the commissioned choreography

✦ the rights and ownership of the choreography

✦ the commencement and conclusion of the contract

✦ the date and location of the first rehearsal and the first performance

✦ the subsistence (often known by the Latin term 'per diem') and travel allowance

✦ payment of fees

✦ the billing (the form and position of your name and credit on all publicity material and printed programmes)

✦ cancellation of contract

✦ revivals, transfers, adaptations and

clauses regarding future use of the choreography

More subjects can and should be considered in an attached *schedule*.

## 3. What is a schedule?

Separate pages, sometimes known as 'the schedule of conditions', may be attached to the main contract for amplification of a clause within it, or to provide space for agreement on other subjects. These may be:

✦ travel arrangements and accommodation abroad or on a tour

✦ taxation (including VAT)

✦ insurance (including National Insurance)

✦ further details of casting, production meetings and rehearsals

✦ dates and locations of further performances

✦ an agreed absence to fulfil a prior engagement

✦ musical matters

✦ sponsorship and publicity matters

✦ your need for an assistant

Contracts, agreements and schedules, along with any alterations or replacement contracts, should be signed and dated by the person authorised to do so on behalf of the commissioning company, and by you 'The Choreographer'. Everyone affected must have a copy. Check that the person signing on behalf of the company is authorised to do so (their official position within the company should be stated under their signature). If in doubt, ask for verification. A witness to your signature does not give a contract any

more legal standing, but it might be useful to be able to prove that another person saw the contract being signed.

## 4. Checking your contract

Reference to many other chapters in this guide will help to ensure that your contract and schedule are comprehensive and cover almost every foreseeable occurrence. *For a convenient list of matters to consider when dealing with contracts or conditions of engagement, in person or by telephone, photocopy the* **Contents Checklist** *(pages xiv–xvii) of this guide and use it for reference.*

When you receive a contract or letter of agreement, notify and consult either your agent, Equity or a legal adviser at the earliest opportunity. Check that the names and addresses of the parties involved are stated clearly. Some companies are popularly known by and operate with one name while also having a different full legal title. For example, 'The Mercury Theatre Trust Ltd' was the full legal name of the Ballet Rambert (now Rambert Dance Company). The full legal name of the company should be used on the contract as well as any trading name. You can check a company's full legal name by telephoning Companies House.

*See also:*
**Useful addresses** (booklet)

Note that in the United Kingdom (England, Wales, Scotland and Northern Ireland) a **fax** is an acceptable legal document. Faxes fade, however, so it is advisable to photocopy onto 'normal' paper any important documents that you receive on fax paper.

Check that the contract states the date on which it commences and the date on which it expires. Check that any written contract or letter of agreement you receive **is** the offer that you were expecting. Remember that any action on your part may indicate acceptance, so question anything you do not agree with straight away **before signing any documents or performing any task** (such as starting rehearsals) which could be taken as an acceptance.

If the management offering you a contract is not known to you, check its credibility with Equity and others. Beware of major organisations unable to offer Equity contracts. Equity publishes a **special attention** list of companies in its journal. Members are urged to contact the Equity office before accepting engagements with companies or individuals listed.

*See also:* **Equity** (page 24)

If you are already employed under contract (perhaps you are a dancer in a company as well as a freelance choreographer), or if you are in training, remember to consult your artistic director, company manager or college principal for permission to accept a contract or invitation to choreograph outside the company or college. If you choreograph a work for your company in the course of your employment, your employer will own the work unless otherwise specified. Secure any agreement in writing. **Always check that all matters relating to the rights and ownership of the choreography are clearly stated.**

*See also:* **Copyright** (page 151)

Check whether you must be exclusively available to the commissioning company, or whether you can undertake other work simultaneously.

It may be possible to commit your services on an exclusive basis for a limited period only: from the beginning of rehearsals to the opening performance, for example. Prior to commencement of rehearsals and after the opening performance you could negotiate a contract which states that you will be available non-exclusively, or on a first-call basis.

Make sure you keep safely at least one copy of any contractual documents you sign.

It is very important to read and understand all clauses in a contract, including those which cover **sickness, dispute, failure to produce, cancellation, arbitration and conciliation**—especially those that appear in small print. If in doubt about any clause, or if you anticipate a problem, consult your agent, Equity or your legal adviser immediately.

## 5. Revivals, transfers and adaptations

In the event of any revival, transfer or adaptation of your work you should be offered a new contract for the altered circumstances, and all matters relating to rights and ownership should be discussed and agreed.

Equity agreements cover transfers of plays and musicals to West End theatres in London. If a production in which your choreography appears does transfer to the West End, you are entitled to additional payment, usually by way of a royalty calculated on gross box office receipts.

*See also:* **Money:**
Royalties and residuals (page 12)

In your original contract you may have given a company the right to perform your choreography for a specific season or period of years. After the expiry of that agreement, in the event of a proposed revival, rights in the choreography will belong to you, and your approval must be sought for any revival if your rights are not to be infringed. A new contract should be negotiated.

Choreographers have sometimes found their names omitted from revival programme credits or chanced upon a revival of their work through the national press in another country. Examples of a management's lack of consultation with the choreographer about revivals seem to have been more prevalent in opera companies, where the choreographer's original contract may not have been sufficiently comprehensive. In these situations, the management's appreciation of the extent of the choreographic contribution, and its view of the choreographer's moral rights and artistic standards, have sometimes proved somewhat shallow. Ideally, the choreographer, or an approved deputy, should be involved in the supervision of any re-staging within this most complex of theatrical forms, unless the original contract specifies an alternative arrangement.

To avoid such incidents it would be advisable to negotiate an agreement in your original contract whereby you are notified if a revival is proposed or scheduled after a specific period, together with the right, or an option, to stage or re-stage any revival or adaptation yourself (subject to your availability).

*See also:*
**Copyright:** Moral rights (page 154)

## 6. If things go wrong

*The telephone rang just as I was closing my suitcase to go to Heathrow. It was the stage manager of the Gran Teatre del Liceu in Barcelona calling me from outside the burning theatre, telling me not to fly to Spain until further notice. By evening the theatre had burnt to a shell. Although the cause of the fire was eventually known to be human error, the management enforced the seventh 'condition' of the contract, which both my agent and I had noted with misgiving before signing the contract but hadn't been able to alter. This 'condition' indemnified the theatre of any responsibility to pay me if unforeseen or unforeseeable circumstances rendered the performances or season suspended. I had already undertaken four weeks administrative and choreographic preparation and was expecting a further month's work. I received no fees or expenses.*

Ann Whitley, choreologist.

The cancellation or withdrawal of a production, or a choreographer's failure to complete a work, may not necessarily be due to the choreographer's short-comings. Consider the following situations:

✦ An industrial dispute, fire, earthquake, riot, epidemic or 'act of god' (action of uncontrollable natural forces) renders the production unachievable and/or the venue ruined. Does your contract protect you against such events? Will you still be paid all or part of your fee? Is the commissioning company exempt from responsibility in such circumstances? (The law in several countries prohibits payment in advance of services—for example France, Italy and Spain).

✦ As a guest choreographer abroad, after some weeks' work you fall ill or are injured and cannot rehearse. The choreography cannot be completed in time for the scheduled first night. You need to fly home for treatment before the conclusion of the contract. You and the management need to resolve your various predicaments amicably and without great financial losses. Is it possible to re-schedule the first performance? Will you have to pay your own flight home because you have inadequate personal business travel insurance and cannot use a pre-paid and dated return flight? What happens to the final part of your fee?

✦ A management accuses you of incompetence or finds your choreographic treatment of a subject offensive. Neither side agrees to compromise. Cancellation or dismissal is threatened. Does your contract make reference to cancellation or dismissal? Are both your financial position and your artistic integrity protected in any way?

✦ On an unscheduled visit to a performance you find that one of your works in the company's repertory has been substantially altered, or you consider the standard of performance consistently poor to the detriment of your work and reputation. Is there a remedy? If not, what are the implications of the withdrawal of your name from the company's printed material and/or the withdrawal of your work from the repertory? Can this be done under the terms of your contract?

You will need qualified professional advice to resolve such situations. Be reassured however that English or Scottish contract law provides considerable protection which may not be specifically described in your contract. Remember that if you are working abroad, local, rather than UK, law may apply, and the written contract will, ideally, state within it which legal system is applicable.

*See also:*
**Insurance:**
The choreographer as freelance artist
*Loss of earnings* (page 150)
*Travel* (page 148)

## 7. Negotiations

> *Sometimes your contract doesn't arrive until you've already started work. One of the problems with this is that any payments due prior to or on the first day of rehearsal are delayed along with the reimbursement of expenses already incurred. Do you **trust** that the company will honour its debts? A video company and a long-established West End director went bankrupt on me. He still drives a Rolls Royce and I never received a penny for the work I did!*
>
> Denni Sayers, choreographer

Much of the advice contained within this chapter would seem to indicate that the process of negotiation normally takes place methodically and that all practical and artistic matters are approached and discussed without meeting any problems. It pre-supposes circumstances in which everyone is absolutely clear about his or her involvement and always available for consultation.

Some choreographers would consider this model ideal, but rare. They advise that a considerable measure of flexibility, generosity, ingenuity, optimism and trust on your part can be an advantage in negotiations. You may well have to weather periods of administrative chaos or vagueness, contradictory information, budget-cutting and project adaptation which may occur before the written contract is issued. These are conditions which do arise from time to time.

There are many circumstances in which choreographers and their assistants have not received a contract (the written

document) at the beginning of the rehearsal period even though negotiations seem to be complete. Despite this guide's advice to get everything in writing as soon as possible, you may find yourself in circumstances where this is impossible or untactful to expect. It would be sensible in these situations to be reassured by your agent or someone in authority that a written contract will be or is being drawn up.

An astute management will research your background and sift information gathered from the professional 'grapevine'. Where there is mutual respect for reputation and working methods between management and choreographer, the period between the invitation to choreograph and the arrival of a written contract is likely to be filled with correspondence, meetings and telephone calls. This period will rely on everyone's best intentions and good will, and there may be much creative anticipation.

Working without a written contract does not necessarily mean that you have no rights. It is often possible to prove evidence of an agreement without a written document, through proof of payment, or documents relating to dates and times of rehearsals.

Whether you agree to begin work on the basis of verbal assurances without the written contract may depend on your professional confidence, your level of trust in the commissioning or producing management, the size and status of that management, and the extent of the preparatory dialogue.

With reference to contractual negotiations, some choreographers have on occasion accepted a job with a much lower fee and status than seemed appropriate under the circumstances.

While acknowledging the danger of underselling themselves, they reflect on some valuable experiences gained by seizing a chance to test their skills, learn more about their craft and work with particular artists or directors.

> *Sometimes it's a question of gaining experience without exploitation, especially while you are learning...*
>
> Quinny Sacks, choreographer

*See also:*

**Agents and managers** (page 19)

**Money** (page 11)

**Insurance** (page 145)

**Equity** (page 24)

**Copyright** (page 151)

**Working as a choreographer:**
Travel arrangements (page 42)
Accommodation arrangements (page 43)
Publicity (page 46)
Making a complaint (page 48)

**Assistants, notators and staff producers** (page 111)

# Money

This chapter draws attention to various aspects of financial management you may have to deal with. The advice in no way represents a comprehensive interpretation of the laws involved. For more detailed information you should consult your agent, Equity, or the government department concerned.

1. Choreographic fee—payment

2. Royalties and residuals

3. Choreographic fee—deductions

4. Expenses:
   *Travel*
   *Accommodation*
   *Subsistence*
   *Incidental*

5. Employment status

6. National Insurance contributions

7. Accountants

8. Unpaid work

9. Union membership

## 1. Choreographic fee—payment

The following are some questions you should ask yourself, your agent or a commissioning management about the payment of your choreographic fee when working in this country or abroad. Ask these questions before you sign the contract:

✦ What is the fee for the created work?

✦ What does that fee represent? Does it include an amount for time spent on any special preliminary research?

✦ For the same fee, are you also required to teach alternative casts during or after the main creative period?

✦ Has a separate fee been negotiated for follow-up or caretaking work at specified venues and dates when the production is on tour?

✦ Is the fee payable in clearly defined instalments—for example, one third on signing the contract, one third on the first day of rehearsals and one third on the day of the première?

✦ Will you be treated as employed or self-employed? Remember that if you are self-employed it will be your responsibility or that of your agent to issue invoices when payment is due.

✦ Will your fee be paid direct to you, to a specified bank account or to your agent or manager?

✦ If working abroad, in which currency will the fee be paid? (Discuss possible fluctuations in currency exchange rates between signing a contract and starting work.)

✦ Are there any restrictions on the amount of money you are permitted to take out of the country in which you will be working?

✦ What are the agreed royalty or residual payment arrangements (if any)?

If you are registered for VAT (Value Added Tax), check that the contract states the fee 'plus VAT'.

Whatever the agreed payment scheme is, if instalments are not being paid exactly as agreed, you may need to visit the finance department (taking your contract with you) to ask when the money **will** be paid to you.

## 2. Royalties and residuals

At present, opera companies do not pay royalties to choreographers (or any other members of the creative team), though they may pay a fee when the work comes back into the repertory after an extended period.

A royalty consists of either a set amount or a negotiated percentage of gross box office receipts. The set sum could be payable for each performance of a work you have created (or in the creation of which you have participated); it could also be a set weekly payment (for a West End musical, for example); or it could be a one-off sum to cover the rights of reproduction which you give the producer in a specific geographical territory or time frame.

For example: you have choreographed a musical which starts in the West End of London. You get a 0.5% (for example) of weekly gross box office takings for the show's run. The show also goes to the USA, where it is reproduced in substantially the same form but you cannot be there to assist in the creation of the 'new' production. The producer pays a one-off sum for your permission to use the original choreography.

Royalties are usually paid weekly, monthly or half-yearly and are accompanied by a certified copy of the box office return for the period in question, or a pay slip indicating the performances covered by the payment. The set sum or percentage amount may rise when the show has recouped its production costs. These facts should be clearly stated in your contract.

Grand rights consist of negotiated sums receivable by the choreographer as creator of an original stage work, depending on the nature and scale of his or her contribution. The sum is based on gross box office takings at the venue, or on the gross sale price paid to the producer.

A residual payment is receivable in return for the rights you grant to the producer to exploit your copyright material in another medium—for instance, television (satellite or cable), video or film. It also applies to sales and repeats of televised material (for instance, an overseas sale by the BBC or a repeated TV commercial).

*See also:*
**Working as a choreographer for television: three examples** (page 79)

If not engaged under an Equity agreement which sets out minimum contractual terms, you should seek qualified professional advice on the royalty and residual scheme or rate offered, and compare notes with colleagues before reaching an agreement. If you do not have an agent, keep all royalty statements safely for Income Tax purposes.

Royalty payments vary greatly according to the commissioning company's budget, the length and nature of the created work, the type of venue at which performances will take place, your professional reputation and the level of your fee. Royalties may be payable from the first performance, or included in the choreographic fee for a specified number of performances. A royalty payment per performance may become payable only upon revival of your work in a company's repertory after a minimum absence of a stated number of months or years.

## 3. Choreographic fee— deductions

It is very important to know which deductions will be made automatically from your fees, and which payments will be your direct responsibility. Deductions should be supported by the appropriate documentation, which you will need for your Income Tax return. Sums deducted will vary from company to company, and from country to country according to the laws and regulations applicable to different kinds of employment.

You are advised to consult your accountant, local inspector of taxes and/ or Equity if planning to work abroad. Many countries have reciprocal tax agreements with the UK, so that tax paid abroad is not paid again at home. Documentary proof of taxes paid is required from either you or your employer. Income earned abroad should always be declared. If no tax has been paid abroad there will be a liability to pay tax on that income on return to the UK. Make sure you have obtained statements of any tax paid before you leave the foreign country.

Sums deducted from your fee could relate to any of the following:

✦ National Insurance (NI) contributions (which can often be avoided when working abroad on presentation of form E101, obtainable from the Department of Social Security Overseas Section, which states that the self-employed individual has an ongoing liability for NI contributions and is therefore exempt from foreign contributions. Obtain before departure and show abroad).

✦ Taxes at the local rate (when working abroad, unless otherwise agreed)

✦ Foreign Withholding Tax (when working abroad unless exemption is obtained).

✦ Tax deducted from your subsistence allowance & travel expenses (abroad)

✦ A compulsory company accident, retirement or medical insurance scheme (as a guest choreographer abroad you may be obliged to contribute a sum).

✦ Union membership fees (see reference later in this chapter)

✦ VAT (particularly in Germany, where some cultural institutions cannot claim VAT and thus have to charge it on fees and expenses paid or deduct it if the individual is not VAT registered).

You will also be responsible for payment of the agreed percentage of your fee to your agent. You should know whether the sum payable to your agent is based on your fee before or after the deduction of any tax or expenses.

## 4. Expenses

A company which issues a letter of agreement or contract may be willing to reimburse you for 'reasonable' expenses. The extent to which any of these expenses are reimbursed will depend on the finances and policy of the commissioning company, or other management, and your 'reasonable' demands, so find out what is meant by 'reasonable'. Compare notes with other members of the creative team. Equity contracts set out their terms and conditions for travel and subsistence expenses which 'may reasonably be incurred'. Find out if you will be paid a flat rate or a sum corresponding to actual expenses supported by receipts and accounts. Most companies insist on actual receipts because of tax problems with flat rate allowances.

*Travel*

✦ Will you, your agent, or the commissioning company or individual make your long-distance travel arrangements even if the commissioning company pays?

✦ What is the reimbursement procedure if you are responsible for making your travel arrangements?

✦ In which currency will you be reimbursed?

✦ When will you buy or receive all the necessary tickets?

✦ How many rail and/or air journeys to and from home are paid for by the company if you are 'commuting'? (The remaining journeys will be made at your expense.)

✦ Has the company agreed a travel rate if you are required to visit the production for cast changes or post-production caretaking?

The company will normally expect you

to pay for taxis to and from the rail or bus station or airport, local taxi fares, parking costs, local bus or underground travel or bicycle hire, for instance, and **may** then reimburse you. Keep all receipts.

*See also:*
**Working as a choreographer:**
Travel arrangements (page 42)

### Accommodation
If you are unable to live at home whilst working for a company, your contract should include the provision of an adequate hotel or apartment while you are working on a project, or an allowance for housing costs. Equity provides guidance on this allowance in the UK. The British Council has a set scale for non-UK venues.

Has the company agreed an accommodation rate for any post-production caretaking which may be necessary if the production goes on tour?

*See also:*
**Working as a choreographer:**
Accommodation arrangements (page 43)

### Subsistence
If you are choreographing a work away from home you will need to know about the daily living allowance ('per diem'), and to assess what that allowance rate might cover. A per diem payment is normally expected to include meals and incidental expenses. If you will be working abroad, Equity maintains a list of British Council recommended subsistence rates.

If working abroad, find out if the living allowance will be subject to tax, and at what rate. Find out when and in which currency you will be paid this allowance. It is most useful to be paid 'on arrival', which usually means at some point during your first day of work. Ask for a receipt.

Has the company agreed a subsistence rate for any caretaking work or post-production visits which may be necessary if the production goes on tour?

### Incidental
'Incidental' expenses are not necessarily small or entirely predictable, and your re-imbursement for certain items will depend on the policy of the company for whom you are working as well as (to a certain extent) the status you hold as a choreographer. The following examples are fairly typical of items and services you will need to pay for, though you should not expect to be reimbursed for all of them:

✦ telephone and fax

✦ photocopying

✦ laundry and dry-cleaning

✦ hire of audio or video recorders for preparatory work

✦ short-term child care

✦ additional local travel costs

✦ notebooks and reference books

✦ gifts for colleagues or cast

## 5. Employment status
Everyone who is paid for work has to account for their earnings at some time or other. They can either be <u>employed</u> or <u>self-employed</u> ('freelance') and it is important to understand the difference. If the Inland Revenue decides that someone has been paid as a freelance/

self-employed person when they should have been paid as an employee, it can demand that the employer pays all the tax and National Insurance due on all previous pay, including the employee's contributions as well as the employer's. This can amount to thousands of pounds and ignorance is no defence.

**For the main considerations involved, see chart on page 18**

The defining factor is the relationship between the organisation and the person, which has to be clear before the contract is agreed. Most cases are easily defined, but some are less clear-cut. If you are in any doubt at all, you should contact your tax office for a ruling. It is not enough for a person to have a Schedule D number because it is quite possible for someone to be employed for one type of work and be freelance at the same time for another. For instance, a dancer could be employed to dance for a company and also be a freelance choreographer.

A common misconception is that someone is freelance if they are working less than full-time. This not true. They could work one hour a week and still be an employee. Similarly, if they are not working on a regular basis, the relationship may still be classified as employment. As far as the Inland Revenue is concerned, a 'casual' is someone who works for a company or organisation for no more than one week in any tax year; anybody else would be an intermittent employee. Even a casual will have to pay National Insurance and tax if the week's pay is more than the relevant thresholds.

There is an anomaly affecting performers who appear in live theatre, opera, dance, or perform in film, video or television. As long as they are not permanent members of the company, they are allowed what is known as 'Reserved Schedule D' status. This means that although they work on a contract of employment, are covered by employment law and pay <u>Class 1</u> NI contributions, they can keep Schedule D status for their tax affairs and do not have tax deducted at source. The PAYE (Pay As You Earn) system copes with these people by allocating them an NT (No Tax) code which the manager has to apply for on special form <u>P46(Ent)</u> when the employment starts.

*See also:* **Equity:** Equity Services (Advice and Rights Guide) (page 26)

It is up to you to tell your local tax office that you are self-employed, wish to have a Schedule D number and which date will be the end of your financial year.

Self-employed people must keep accurate records of the dates and amounts they have been paid for every job they do, along with records of tax and NI deductions, unemployment benefit, income support, royalty and residual payments, and expense claims and reimbursements. A numbered triplicate invoice book, available from office stationers, makes record-keeping easier. A spreadsheet package for a computer is also very efficient. Both methods will leave you with detailed copies of the income and expenditure accounts you should submit to various bodies, and a secure source of reference for the future.

## 6. National Insurance contributions

Everyone in the United Kingdom, from age 16 to 65 (or 60 for women) is liable to pay National Insurance contributions. In order to qualify for some state benefits (including the retirement pension) a certain amount of contributions have to be paid, and it is illegal not to do so whilst working. However, some married women can choose to pay at a reduced rate, although their benefit entitlement is reduced as a result. Employees in a company pension scheme which has been 'contracted out' also pay lower contributions.

Contributions fall into four classes, depending on whether you are self-employed or an employee. The amount you are liable to pay is directly related to the amount you earn in any given week. Basic <u>Class 2</u> contributions can be paid by direct debit on a form for this purpose available from your local DSS (Department of Social Security) office. The balance owing is usually paid as <u>Class 4</u> contributions together with your Income Tax (if you are self-employed).

## 7. Accountants

Many people keep their own detailed financial records and complete their own Income Tax return at the end of each financial year. Self-employed people earning less than £15,000 per year (1995) are allowed to submit very simple three-line accounts. However, some people prefer to rely on the services of an accountant. He or she will ensure that your entitlement to all deductions and tax relief is documented. An accountant will charge fees for the amount of time he or she spends attending to your affairs so it is important to keep accurate and accessible records of income and expenses to reduce the amount of work your accountant may have to do and so keep your payment to him or her as low as possible. An accountant will require you to submit your financial details promptly according

to an agreed scheme.

The Inland Revenue can investigate your tax affairs up to six years in arrears. It is therefore very important to keep accounts, bank statements, pay slips, receipts, invoices and any other paperwork in an efficient filing system for the required amount of time before throwing them away.

## 8. Unpaid work

There may be occasions when you choose to work without payment (for example, voluntary teaching or working for a charity). It is still good practice to keep a record for tax purposes of time spent and expenses incurred and/or reimbursed.

## 9. Union membership

Check that your Equity or other relevant professional body's annual membership fee is paid to ensure that help is available if difficulties arise. These organisations can often help with free legal advice from lawyers who understand the performing arts world.

*See also:*
**Working abroad** (page 103)
**Contract** (page 3)
**Agents and managers** (page 19)

| Employed = an employee | Self-Employed = a freelance |
|---|---|
| Has one main job, with maybe a couple of other things on the side N.B. none of these has to be full-time | Has many jobs with different organisations |
| The organisation can tell them what to do and when to do it ie a 'master/servant' relationship exists | The organisation can specify the end product of the services but can't tell the person what to do or when to do it |
| Works agreed hours e.g. Mon-Fri, 10-6 or so many hours in the week | Can decide own working hours as long as the job is done in time |
| Works in a space i.e. office or studio, paid for by the organisation | Works in a space they pay for themselves |
| Uses equipment provided and/or paid for by the organisation e.g. costumes, make-up for dancers, computer/printer for administrator etc. | Uses equipment they provide and/or pay for themselves |
| Organisation pays phone bill | Freelance pays own phone bill; organisation my reimburse for specific calls if in contract |
| Organisation pays stationery and postage | Freelance pays own stationery and postage; organisation my reimburse for specific items if in contract |
| Organisation pays for travel between base and work site but not between home and base | Freelance pays all travel; organisation my reimburse for specific journeys if in contract |
| Paid a wage or salary calculated by the hour, day week or month | Paid a fixed fee for the job |
| May be able to claim overtime if works more than agreed hours | Can't claim overtime; own responsibility if goes over time allotted for job |
| Paid on the agreed pay day and given a pay slip | Often paid in instalments e.g. upon signing contract and on first night |
| Can be paid when off ill if agreed in contract | Doesn't get paid if ill |
| Qualifies for holiday pay if a greed in contract | Doesn't get paid when on holiday |
| Has a contract of service or employment | Has a contract for services |
| Has to pay tax on PAYE (Schedule E) | Has to pay tax on Schedule D |
| Is paid with tax deducted at source | Is paid gross with no deduction for tax |
| Pays National Insurance Class 1 contributions deducted at source; employer has to pay Employer's NI on top | Has to pay National Insurance Class 2 contributions every week and then also Class 4 at the end of the year as a percentage of profits |
| Has to give name, address, NI number and P45 (or sign P46) at start of employment, then can be paid without any more paperwork | Has to issue invoice(s), preferably numbered, showing name, address, phone and Schedule D number, every time they want to be paid |
| Protected by contract law and employment law | Protected by contract law |

# Agents and managers

Whilst choreographers often find work through particular relationships they have formed with individual directors, producers and companies over a period of time, many find an agent or manager very useful. There are many types of agent and/or manager and you may encounter many different working relationships.

1. What is an agent or manager?

2. How to find an agent-manager

3. The initial meeting

4. What an agent-manager may or may not do

5. What an agent-manager expects from you

6. Changing agent-managers

7. Other management and production services

## 1. What is an agent or manager?

An agent is someone who may get you work for a percentage of your earnings. He or she can be a manager or a booking agent. A booking agent keeps your diary up to date, answers telephone enquiries, sends out your biography and photographs, forwards contracts to you, and generally acts as a secretary. For this a 10% (or more) commission (plus VAT) is taken from your fee for work performed in the UK, and a larger percentage commission for work abroad.

An agent-manager guides a career: firstly, a relationship is formed with the artist, and a sensible course of action is discussed. What are your strengths? What do you need to work on? What do you want to be doing in 10 years time? Whose work do you admire? He or she will also try to arrange meetings with certain directors you would like to approach, give you advice on the fees you should be charging and help you with strategies for moving your career into new areas. As with a booking agent, a 10% (or more) commission (plus VAT) is taken for work performed in the UK. An agent-manager should combine both these functions.

## 2. How to find an agent-manager

Lists of managers and agents of good standing are kept by Equity, Spotlight (in the 'Contacts' directory), the British Council and other professional bodies. Other lists may be found in dance, music, theatre and opera directories, yearbooks or handbooks, which are often available at your local library. Agents and managers will often be members of a business association—for example, the Personal Managers' Association or the British

Association of Concert Agents. Word of mouth is often the best way to identify a good manager. If your colleagues are well represented by a certain individual or agency, then that is a good place to start.

*See also:*
**Useful publications** (booklet)
**Useful addresses** (booklet)

It is helpful if you already have a job offer. Agent-mangers, however, will not necessarily be tempted by the lure of money, and will want to know you and your work to enable a working relationship to develop. As an artist, don't be tempted to take the first agent's offer. If speed really is essential, but you don't want to be pressured into choosing someone immediately, then ask a reputable agent to negotiate the contract for you on a one-off basis for a fee or commission. If there is no work to negotiate but you have a production coming up, inform every agent you know of about it—about a month in advance.

Find out what you can about the agent before writing and address the person by name. It may be relevant and of interest to know about the number and range of professionals he or she represents: would you be the only choreographer on the agent's books or one of several?

There is little point trying to get an agent if there is no work to see, so don't 'cold call' unless you are already well-known. There is nothing much apart from an existing production upon which an agent can make a judgement.

Having issued the invitation, follow up about a week later with a telephone call. If the invitation is accepted, make sure you have a ticket waiting and that the agent knows where it will be waiting for collection, and whose name it will have on the envelope—yours or his or hers. Look after the agent at the show—an interval drink, or merely introducing yourself, is a sensible move.

After the agent has been to see the show, wait a week and then call again. At that point the agent may ask to meet to talk about your career and aspirations. The agent may want to see some other work you have coming up—this is not prevarication as much as the need to see a range of your choreography.

## 3. The initial meeting

Take visual material in a portfolio, and try to send a video or showreel in advance. Talk through a production of which you are particularly proud—how you got the commission, how you chose the dancers, what your brief was, how you approached it and how you chose or collaborated with other members of the creative team.

Be precise and ask all the questions you want. Make a list before you go to the meeting. Ask about the agent's other clients and what his or her 'philosophy of management' may be. A busy agent will probably give you half an hour to an hour. Finish your interview by establishing what happens next: who is going to be in touch with whom, and whether any additional material is required.

Go and meet at least three other managers before you make your choice.

## 4. What an agent-manager may or may not do

An agent only rarely gets work for a client by ringing around all his or her contacts and asking what work is available. His or her job is to keep an ear to the ground and make sure your name is in front of the producer when a decision to engage a choreographer is made.

Your agent-manager will probably not handle your book-keeping—Income Tax, National Insurance contributions and VAT returns—but may be able to help by recommending an accountant. However, the manager will invoice producers for your fees (plus VAT), process the cheques, invoice you for commission (plus VAT) and provide you with a statement. You have to keep up your Equity and any other professional subscriptions.

The client should expect the agent-manager to deal with all contractual matters—fees, expenses, travel payments, subsistence, copyright and billing (programme credits and the position and form of your name on publicity material). Most contracts follow standard patterns, but it is essential to have an agent in whom you have absolute confidence to negotiate for you. Things you may not see as important—exclusive and non-exclusive performance rights, residual payments, film rights, reproductions, foreign sales—are what agent-managers look out for and know how to include in contracts. Make sure that you are fully involved in the discussions so that you are not taken by surprise at a later date. An agent-manager will expect to undertake a certain amount of administrative work such as booking flights and hotels, arranging for someone to meet you at the airport, arranging work permits and visas.

In the case of a complex West End musical or a three act production for a big foreign company, the contract can take months to negotiate and involve lawyers as well as producer and agent-manager. Your agent-manager may ask you if you would like a solicitor to look over your contract in such an instance, to check the precise interpretation of the wording. Negotiate with your agent how fees for this kind of professional advice are to be paid—by the two of you or by one party alone.

An agent-manager can often advise about whether to accept a job or not: if currently very short of money, your inclination might be to take on anything offered, regardless of suitability. Your agent-manager should make a dispassionate judgement on whether this fits in with your career plan. You can also expect help when your career seems to be stuck in a groove—always working with the same director, for example, or only doing movement in drama, when you really want to move into musicals. Your agent-manager should be aware if you are being over-stretched, taking on too big a piece of work without an assistant, or trying to do two projects at once.

An agent-manager is usually very happy to discuss an artist's career, and to make suggestions and positive criticisms at the same time. As a client, you have the right to expect your manager's full concentration (but not every single day of the week).

## 5. What an agent-manager expects from you

The agent-manager will expect hard work in return for his or her investment of time, energy and money in a young artist. In the long run, that investment will pay off, and he or she will earn money from the work that the artist brings in.

Your agent-manager will need to know who you have been talking to about your work. A dinner party is not necessarily the best place to hand out a biography, but your agent-manager can do that for you the next day. Most work comes through your own personal contacts. If you have had a good working relationship with a certain director then it is as much up to you as your manager to keep the contact going. You must expect to hustle on your own behalf, not just rely on the agent-manager to find you work.

Above all, keep in touch. Don't go off for a month's holiday without telling your manager. He or she will only be frustrated at not being able to contact you when a big job offer comes in. Keep your agent-manager up to date with your diary.

## 6. Changing agent-managers

As a rule, artists do not change management at the start and the end of their careers. At the start you need a manager more than a management needs you, and at the end there is little point in change for its own sake. However, at some stage you may decide to leave your agent-manager for one who has different contacts, is more sympathetic or is able to give a more personal service. Such a move should be carefully handled.

## 7. Other management and production services

There are many organisations which exist alongside the agent-manager system described above. These are usually independent production companies or administration-based organisations which fulfil some of the services of an agent-manager, either for the period of a production or on a long-term basis. Artists affiliated with such organisations may use them alongside an agent-manager, or may use them for a certain area of work (artists may be affiliated with an arts administration organisation, for example, for their more experimental work whilst their agent-manager looks after the day-to-day side of their affairs). These organisations offer an alternative to the agent-manager system, and often have a different set of criteria upon which they decide to work with artists. Such organisations do not, however, have ever-open books, and their capacity to serve a large number of artists is limited.

*See also:*
**Contract** (page 3)
**Money** (page 11)

# Equity

British Actors' Equity, generally known as <u>Equity</u>, is a trade union for performers, directors, choreographers, designers and other non-technical entertainment industry professionals. Its principal function is to secure the best possible terms and conditions for its members in professional employment through collective bargaining, and to represent individuals or groups of members in disputes with employers in the course of their employment.

1. Equity/Theatrical Management Association (TMA) Agreement

2. Equity/Society of London Theatre (SOLT) Agreement

3. Contract details

4. Equity services

5. Choreographers' Register

6. Choreographers' Committee

Equity has three departments covering the spread of the entertainment industry —theatre, variety and film and television & radio. In addition to its head office in London, Equity has offices in Cardiff, Glasgow and Manchester. Staff in each of these locations give specific advice and help when members are working in the geographical areas covered by these offices.

In order to be eligible to join Equity, a choreographer needs to be able to provide proof—in the form of contracts (Equity or non-Equity), publicity and press notices—of his or her regular payment from professional activities.

At present Equity has two agreements for choreographers; the Equity/TMA Agreement for Choreographers in theatres using the Subsidised Repertory and Provincial Commercial contracts, and the Equity/SOLT Agreement for West End Theatre Choreographers. A summary is given here:

## 1. Equity/Theatrical Management Association (TMA) Agreement

In recognition of the diversity of subsidised repertory theatres, each one is assigned to one of four Middle Range Salary Levels. For example, a major subsidised theatre such as Nottingham Playhouse is assigned to MRSL 1, while a Theatre in Education company attached to a smaller repertory company could be assigned to MRSL 4. Minimum fees paid to choreographers reflect this categorisation. Distinctions also exist between the scale of production in commercial theatre.

You will come across the terms higher minimum and lower minimum. Higher minimum is the default scale of pro-

duction. A producer must satisfy at least four out of six criteria defined in the performers' Provincial Theatre Agreement to be able to make payment at the lower rate. Equity will advise you of the MRSL grade of a theatre or of the status of a commercial theatre producer. If in doubt, check with Equity before negotiations are too advanced.

The minimum fee covers up to three days of pre-production work, auditions and casting and a maximum of two weeks' rehearsal. Additional weeks of rehearsal are paid at a minimum weekly rate, while further days of pre- or post-production attract a further daily rate. You can also be engaged on a daily rate for a maximum of six days.

## 2. Equity/Society of London Theatre (SOLT) Agreement

This agreement draws distinctions between choreography and/or musical staging for musicals or plays, and a small amount of choreography/staging for plays. Minimum fees and the commitment required of a choreographer vary accordingly. For example, the fee for a major musical covers a maximum of six days pre-production and auditioning and up to five weeks' rehearsal. A fee for a play covers three days' pre-production attendance and up to 18 days attendance over a period of five consecutive weeks for rehearsal. Additional weeks of rehearsal for a musical are paid at a weekly rate, while additional work on a play can be paid for by the session. In both cases, minimum weekly royalties are specified.

A small amount of choreography or musical staging can be undertaken on a session basis, although it is important to note that you must also be called for at least the technical and dress rehearsals and two performances (one of which can be the press night). A royalty payment is not guaranteed in this type of engagement, although SOLT recognises that in certain circumstances a royalty may be appropriate, depending on the impact and importance of the choreography or staging within the production as a whole. This is the intention of the clause in the agreement which specifies that a weekly royalty 'may be negotiated'.

Both agreements mentioned above specify minimum rates for assistant choreographers. Equity also have agreements for choreographers with both the BBC and ITV.

## 3. Contract details

There are specimens of the standard contract for choreographers engaged for productions in the West End theatre, the standard contract for assistant choreographers engaged for productions in the West End theatre and the standard contract for theatre choreographers in provincial commercial and subsidised repertory theatre in the booklet enclosed with this guide.

TMA and SOLT members are required to issue the corresponding standard forms of engagement. If you are offered work by an employer who belongs to one of these management bodies and you do not receive a standard contract, get in touch with Equity. These contracts have clauses which specify arrangements for royalty payments, copyright and so forth, and it is important therefore that the contract is used to ensure your minimum rights are not infringed. It is also import-ant to have a standard contract in the

event of a dispute with your employer.

On the specimen contract you will see that it is deemed to incorporate all the provisions of the schedule, which contains the detailed clauses taken from agreement booklets. Copies of the agreements are available from Equity head office. If you are offered a contract which varies the terms of the agreements, and you have not agreed to these changes, get in touch with Equity.

## 4. Equity services

The relationship between subsidised theatre and commercial theatre is becoming more complex, as commercial and subsidised managers enter into co-productions involving an initial season in repertory, a national UK tour, and a transfer of the work to a West End theatre. Make sure the producer is aware that each stage of a production similar to the above example will have implic-ations for you in terms of the contracts which will define your rights.

Equity will take up disputes arising on your behalf, referring if necessary to a hearing of the London or Provincial Theatre Councils, which are the theatre industry's arbitration and conciliation forums.

Equity can offer you advice in areas not covered by existing contracts, as many of the issues involved in neg-otiating a contract are common to all areas of work. The organisation will also advise you on overseas contracts, tax, National Insurance, general and travel insurance and welfare benefits matters, and offers a valuable legal service to members in contract disputes and personal injury cases.

Equity publishes an Advice and Rights Guide, available free to members. Make sure your union subscriptions are up-to-date to ensure you receive each revised copy. This publication will guide you through the complexities of state benefits and offer advice on several areas covered in this Guide, such as tax, National Insurance and work abroad. If you need specialist advice, get in touch with Equity's Welfare Benefits Adviser.

*See also:*
**Useful publications** (booklet)

Equity publishes a quarterly journal, free to members, containing news and information on current developments within the union. This journal also contains a special attention list, which indicates employers and organisations with whom Equity has had unsatisfactory dealings. If you are offered work by any employer on the list, get in touch with Equity immediately. It may save you a lot of time, money and energy to know in advance that an employer has outstanding debts or court judgements against them.

## 5. Choreographers' Register

The agreements outlined above are periodically re-negotiated and improvements are sought for pay and other contractual conditions. At a time of great change in theatre, and indeed in other media, it is important that you keep Equity advised of your experiences as a working choreographer. Equity has a Choreographers' Register (open to any choreographer member) which is kept informed of changes to agreements, and consulted in the preparation of claims for improvements to existing contracts.

## 6. Choreographers' Committee

Choreographers are represented within

Equity by the Choreographers' Committee, which is elected by members of the Choreographers' Register every two years. The committee, which has representatives from the widest range of the dance world, is keen to establish standard contracts in all areas of the industry currently covered by Equity. The committee also received the backing of the membership in seeking a specialist seat on the Equity Council, the Union's governing body, to assist in the better representation of professional choreographers in the industry.

*See also:*
**Useful addresses:**
national and regional Equity offices (booklet)

PART **2**

# PART 2

## Working as a choreographer

# Working as a choreographer

This chapter addresses many aspects of the preparation, creation and care of your choreography, and the need to keep your creative process well-supported. The subjects addressed here should serve as a checklist of topics from which you can choose those which apply to your particular work, whether it is large or small-scale, for a dance, opera or film company, in theatre or in education.
Many other chapters in this guide will direct you back to this chapter for reference.

1. **The choreography:**
   *Title*
   *Length*
   *Full evening works and mixed programmes*
   *Other movement specialists*
   *First and future performances*

2. **Rehearsals:**
   *Time to create the work*
   *Schedules*
   *Clashing engagements*
   *Facilities—checklist*
   *Props*
   *Personal equipment*

3. **Pre- and post production meetings**

4. **Casting:**
   *Adults*
   *Children*
   *Guest artists*
   *Availability of performers*
   *Animals and birds*

5. **Audition procedure**

6. **Travel arrangements**

7. **Accommodation arrangements**

8. **Administrative tasks:**
   *Personal details*
   *Company information*
   *A seat for the first performance*
   *Security pass*

9. **Publicity**

10. **Programme credits:**
    *Choreographer and choreography*
    *Cast and other contributors*
    *Sponsor and funding body*
    *Checklist*

11. **Making a complaint**

12. **Transfers: consultation with the production team**

## 1. The choreography

### Title

You may be invited to choreograph a new work, or sections of choreography which form part of a new or larger revised production. At such a preliminary stage in the negotiations you might feel unable to define what the finished work will be, and you may be reluctant to provide a title. Be aware, however, of the press and marketing department's need to know the title of your work as soon as possible.

If you are pressed to provide a title before the choreography's development has begun, reserve the right to change a provisional name stated in the contract if it is clearly referred to as a 'working title'. Find out the deadline for the final title. Check the exact spelling, and any accents and translation of non-English words. Consider whether a sub-title would be an appropriate accompaniment.

### Length

Find out if the length of the choreography is your decision. If the decision lies with someone else, such as the composer, find out if there are any constraints on your work's length. Does the exact duration depend on the length of a commissioned musical score?

*See also:* **Music:**
Commissioned music (page 123)

### Full evening works and mixed programmes

If you plan a so-called full length work, find out which other works will make up the company's repertory whilst your work is in rehearsal and performance. It could be an advantage to have some details, as many aspects of a repertory or touring

company's work could affect your process and progress as a guest choreographer.

When choreographing a work as part of a triple bill, for example, it should be established where in the running order your work will appear, and when any intervals will take place. If you have definite ideas about the nature and placing of your proposed work, make them clear to the company at an early stage. If other newly-created works are to be performed in the same programme, the running order and the expectations of the commissioning management and all choreographers should be agreed as far in advance as possible.

The balance, contrast and smooth-running of a mixed bill will depend on several factors:

✦ casting (especially where dancers are performing in two or more works)

✦ design and lighting

✦ music or sound sources

✦ staging and technical considerations

✦ the nature of each work

Check in your discussions whether your or your lighting designer's plans may be conditioned by a limited rig which has already been designed to accommodate the needs of other works.

*See also:* **Lighting design** (page 136)

### Other movement specialists

There may be occasions when you invite a movement specialist to work with you on a production. Or, if you are choreographing a work which will form part of a new or revised production, you may discover that other choreographers will be involved. These may be a fight director, gymnast, stunt director, ballroom or folk dance expert, or a specialist in a non-western form of dance or dance-drama. You will want to meet your collaborators, to know what collaboration is possible (think about casting and rehearsal schedules), and that your areas of choreographic responsibility have been defined.

See also:
**Working as a choreographer in opera and musical theatre:**
Other choreographers or movement specialists (page 55)
Rehearsal sessions (page 57)

*First and future performances*
The date and place of the first performance should be stated in your contract. The commissioning company may also discuss with you the possible use of your finished work in the future. Are you working for a resident or touring company? This and other questions may considerably affect your planning, as well as that of your designer:

✦ How many performances are planned to follow the first one?

✦ Are any performances scheduled on Sundays or national holidays?

✦ Will your work form part of the company's repertory for a limited period?

✦ Will the choreography need to be adapted to suit a variety of venues (thrust or open-air stages for example) whilst on tour?

✦ Will the set need to be adapted for touring to a variety of venues?

✦ Will your work be in repertory for a season with the possibility of a transfer to a West End or other theatre? (If this is the case, refer to **Transfers: consultation with the production team** later in this chapter.)

*See also:*
**Contract:**
Revivals, transfers and adaptations (page 6)

**Copyright** (page 151)

**Set and costume design** (page 130)

**Money:**
Royalties and residuals (page 12)

# 2. Rehearsals

*Time to create the work*
The amount of rehearsal time required or available to you needs to be confirmed at the start of negotiations. Will other works be rehearsed and given stage calls during the same period as your work is rehearsed and staged? These conditions may affect the amount of studio and stage time you are allocated. Make sure that sufficient sessions are scheduled to facilitate the transition from rehearsal studio to stage or performing area. Do not underestimate the magnitude of this adjustment, especially for large-scale productions.

The date of your first rehearsal should be stated in your contract. Ask for a complete production schedule listing the following details, or ask to be informed in writing as soon as each detail is fixed:

✦ the number of studio rehearsal sessions in each week available to you

✦ the number of weeks available to you

33

in the studio

+ the number of rehearsals with full cast

+ the date and time of stage rehearsals with piano (or other) accompaniment

+ the date and time of stage rehearsals with recorded music, ensemble, band, orchestra (or other) accompaniment

+ the date and time of technical rehearsals with or without performers

+ the date and time of rehearsals in partial or full costume, wigs and make-up

+ the date and time of rehearsals with an 'indicated', partial or full set

+ the date and time of rehearsals with special effects

+ the date and time of lighting rehearsals

+ the date and time of the dress (or 'general') rehearsal(s)

+ the date and time of any preview performances

Ask if the dress rehearsal will be open to the public, and whether press photographers will be present.

It is important in an early stage in your enquires to check that none of the following will (as far as can be predicted) obstruct your rehearsal period:

+ company free days

+ bank, city or national holidays

+ local festivals

+ local or national industrial disputes (postal, sea port, transport)

*See also:* **Contract** (page 3)

## Schedules

As a guest choreographer you will need to know the local pattern and length of rehearsal sessions (and breaks) and which are scheduled for your use. Are performers contracted to work for four, five or six days a week? For how long can they work each day? Find out whether your performers work, for example, either morning and afternoon or morning and evening. If, for example, performers are only allowed to work a maximum of two sessions per working day, **you** might decide to work three sessions in order to maximise your time with different groups or individuals.

The time of day scheduled for your rehearsals is likely to have some affect upon your progress. Most dancers are more receptive immediately after morning class, so try not to have all your rehearsals at the end of the day when dancers may be tired or thinking about the evening's performance.

Find out about regulations applicable to overtime and weekend work.

If you are not drafting your own rehearsal schedules, find out who is responsible for writing, co-ordinating and supplying them to all departments. Make your requirements known and find out on which day schedules are drafted, on which day they are issued, and where they are displayed and distributed.

It is important to be aware of regulations relating to timetable alterations and notice of intention to alter the timetable for all ranks of performers. These may vary from company to company and country to country. If you propose a draft timetable, covering several weeks of rehearsal involving various groups and casts of performers, and you send it as requested to a company (perhaps abroad), alterations by telephone and fax made in advance in accordance with the regulations may be possible. Plans to alter the timetable on your arrival, in the light of unforeseen circumstances, may not be permitted. Minor changes may be possible. Remember that timetable changes often affect many different departments or individuals within a company.

The weekly schedule issued by a large ballet or opera company operating a repertory system is likely to be densely packed with a variety of information and can be difficult to interpret. It is very important to identify that all your rehearsals and breaks are scheduled. Ask for help if you are in any doubt, especially when working abroad. The lay-out of the schedule will vary from company to company. Check that you understand code numbers and abbreviations, as well as initials used to refer to studios, artists or staff.

*See also:*
**Working as a choreographer in opera and musical theatre:**
Rehearsal sessions (page 57)

*Clashing engagements*
You should check in your contract to see whether it states that you must be exclusively available to the commissioning company. If you are able to accept two overlapping engagements in different places, consider the practical, creative, domestic, health and travel implications.

*See also:* **Contract** (page 3)

*Facilities—checklist*
Rehearsal facilities vary greatly from company to company and city to city. A company management or local authority's

assurance that its rehearsal facilities are good may prove to be true, but it is always worth making some polite enquiries, especially when working with a management that is unfamiliar with the needs of dancers or people who dance. In this way you will either be reassured that the conditions are, indeed, good, or you will sense a need to visit the studio or hall before agreeing to rehearse there. Your priorities as a choreographer and the needs of your cast as far as rehearsal conditions are concerned are likely to be affected by the nature and scale of the choreography, the climate, and your or the commissioning company's budget. You may find the following checklist helpful in a variety of circumstances:

✦ Where, exactly, will rehearsals take place? Which studio in which building?

✦ Are the rehearsal studios within easy reach of the theatre, performance venue or administrative offices you may also need to use?

✦ Are the studios available for your or your production's exclusive use? (You may like to prepare yourself or prepare work before rehearsals begin.)

✦ Has another organisation booked the studio at night?

✦ Are all the dimensions of the studio adequate for your purposes? (Don't forget to check that you have a working height clear of any wooden beams, metal girders or light fittings.)

✦ Are there any pillars that will obstruct your working space?

✦ Is the studio floor sprung? Who could give you more information about its construction?

✦ Does the floor surface provide the right qualities of slip, grip or comfort for your purposes? Is it suitable for pointe shoes, bare feet, soft shoes, heeled boots or tap shoes?

✦ If the floor construction is suitable, but the surface is unsuitable, can a dance floor be laid and left there for the duration of your rehearsals? (Beware of the dangers of concrete, carpets and rough wood.)

✦ If a floor needs to be installed, who will do this and when?

✦ Is rosin available? May your dancers use it on the existing floor? Is there a rosin tray?

✦ What are the nightly or weekly cleaning arrangements, and what detergents are normally used to clean the floor?

✦ Are you, or stage management, allowed to use floor marking tape, and can the tape be left there each night?

✦ Can sections of the set, pieces of furniture and rostra be semi-permanently fixed (screwed in) to the floor and left for the duration of your rehearsals? Will certain items have to be moved before classes or warm-ups? Is the designer involved in these questions?

✦ Do you require a studio with wall barres or portable barres?

✦ Do you require mirrors and/or blackout facilities?

✦ If using a piano, has it been tuned recently and is it in full working order? Is there a piano stool or suitable chair?

✦ Can large items such as a piano, musical equipment or portable barres be transported from the street or car park to the rehearsal studio? Is there a large enough lift in working order? How narrow are the stairs? What are the dimensions of the doorways?

✦ Is there good access for disabled performers or staff who may have limited mobility? (If there is a lift, check its suitability for a wheelchair.)

✦ Can you park near the studio?

✦ Can the studio be reached by public transport? Can you get home by public transport late at night?

✦ Are the studios adequately heated and ventilated? Are the studios heated at weekends?

✦ Is the light source natural or artificial?

✦ What activities take place in the vicinity of the studio? (If the windows are open and the studio adjoins a busy construction site, you may have persistent noise, smell and dust problems.)

✦ What sort of male and female changing rooms, washing and showering facilities are available to you and your cast and staff (including disabled members)? Are the facilities cleaned on a regular basis?

✦ Are there good canteen facilities available to suit all tastes? Are these facilities open throughout your rehearsal period? Are there any alternatives nearby?

✦ Is there a rest area or 'Green Room' with a power socket? Are there smoking and non-smoking areas?

✦ Is there a hot and cold water supply and drinking water available?

✦ Is there a first aid kit?

✦ Is there somewhere that icepacks can be kept frozen?

✦ Are there any public telephones in the building? If not, are there some nearby?

✦ Is there somewhere to keep valuables secure?

✦ Is there a security guard, doorkeeper, warden, or caretaker on duty? What hours do they keep?

✦ Are there adequate power sockets in each studio for audio and visual equipment?

✦ If you are not providing your own audio or visual equipment, check on the availability of any equipment provided by the studio and its compatibility with your tapes and videotapes.

✦ If you are using a video recorder to document your work does the company have a camera person to work with you and for how long will he or she be available to work with you each day?

✦ If some of your rehearsals will take place in another studio, is it big enough, and are the facilities adequate for your cast?

If you are going to pay for the rehearsal space:

✦ Have you been given the necessary schedule of costs, including any reduced terms for weekly or longer hire?

✦ Is audio/visual equipment part of the studio hire or is there an additional fee?

✦ If acceptable and affordable, what are the rental and payment arrangements?

*See also:*
**Health and safety** (page 156)

**Insurance** (page 145)

**Useful publications:**
*A Handbook for Dance Floors* (booklet)
*Dance Spaces* (booklet)

## Props

Will it be important to have floor markings, props, items of furniture or set or items of costume available at rehearsals? Try to make your requests known to the relevant departments well in advance of the day on which you need them.

Would it be helpful to have copies of a synopsis, vocal or choral text, or other reference material available for the cast on the first day of rehearsals?

*See also:* **Set and costume design:**
Items for rehearsal—checklist (page 133)

## Personal equipment

Before you start rehearsals, check that you have all the equipment and materials you need for the length of your employment

✦ Have you got all the necessary music, libretti, text or scripts? Has each one been marked with cuts and/or additions?

✦ If you are providing your own CD, video or cassette player, have you got enough charged batteries, cables, leads and spare tapes (note that whilst working abroad you may find it difficult to get the same type of battery)?

✦ Have you got all necessary videos, cassettes or CDs?

✦ Have you got copies of all the necessary designs and photographs?

✦ Have you got all necessary schedules and cast lists?

✦ Have you got the company's personnel list?

✦ Have you got a first aid kit?

✦ Will you need to take your own food and drink?

✦ If you are working in a different or unpredictable climate, do you have enough warm and/or cool rehearsal clothes and shoes?

Note that some dancers and other performers find it difficult to see or 'read' a choreographer's movement, particularly the detail, if large enveloping sweatshirts are worn, or if the choreographer is dressed in one overall dark colour.

## 3. Pre- and post-production meetings

At pre- and post-production meetings, many departments involved in a production may come together to discuss and check that technical, artistic and administrative aspects of the production are running smoothly and according to schedule. It is in these meetings that potential difficulties come to light and are often ironed out. The different departments or individuals involved in these meetings may be:

✦ Artistic director
✦ Finance and administration

✦ Press, publications and marketing
✦ Rehearsal director
✦ Notator and/or personal assistant
✦ Education
✦ Children's manager
✦ Video maker and/or operator
✦ Conductor, musical director, musical staff
✦ Chorus master
✦ Set designer(s)
✦ Costume designer(s)
✦ Shoes, wigs, millinery staff
✦ Lighting designer
✦ Sound engineer or designer
✦ Stage management
✦ Technical management
✦ Props
✦ Special effects

Consider the following:

✦ What is the status of each individual in the over-all production?

✦ Have you discussed mutually satisfactory arrangements for meetings with the different departments, or has the company informed you of the schedule of proposed dates, times and locations?

✦ Is there a prescribed number of pre- and post-production meetings stated in your contract?

✦ If you want to call a meeting, do you know who to contact in order to set the process in motion?

✦ Is everyone who should be involved available?

✦ Will the model of the set be available at specified meetings?

✦ If you are unable to attend any scheduled meetings, should you send an informed deputy? Have you informed the company?

✦ Who will write up production meeting decisions and distribute the information?

✦ If your contract makes no reference to a post-dress rehearsal or post-first night meeting, would it be wise to ask in advance for one (or both) to be scheduled and for you to be informed if this is possible? If it is possible, who (ideally) should attend?

✦ Is reimbursement available for reasonable travel and subsistence expenses incurred to attend meetings? (This should be stated in your contract.)

*For a convenient list of matters to consider in pre- and post production meetings, photocopy the* **Contents Checklist** *(pages xiv–xvii) of this guide.*

If, as a choreographer-director, you have spent some weeks or months speculating on the feasibility of a project—perhaps a relatively low budget production which is still at the discussion stage but which, nevertheless, has involved a number of 'supporters'—don't forget to notify all concerned if the proposed project has to be abandoned or postponed. In these circumstances, dancers may be standing by, and there may be others who have supported your venture by giving free advice and time on the understanding that they will be involved in the project.

*See also:*

**Set and costume design:**
Discussions with the designer (page 131)
The model (page 132)

**Lighting design:**
What do you need? (page 137)

# 4. Casting

*Adults*

The casting of your choreography could be exclusively your choice or it could be by mutual agreement with the company's artistic director. Find out in advance which arrangement will prevail and make known any particular needs or wishes. If you wish to retain tight control over casting decisions for a specified period, you should make your wishes known in writing.

Find out about the casting procedures in standard contracts and assess how they might affect you.

If you are not familiar with the commissioning company's style and the talent of individual performers, you could ask to attend rehearsals and performances or see company videotapes in advance of your engagement.

Some further questions you may need to ask yourself and others:

✦ Is there a maximum or minimum number of dancers you can use?

✦ Have you been invited to include named company members? Do you know their work?

✦ Do you intend to begin work before final casting decisions are made? Is the company in agreement?

You should be aware of any time limits for casting decisions, as there will be wardrobe, press and marketing departments waiting for a decision.

Discuss decisions concerning alternative casts. If by mutual agreement you have established several casts for a specified period of performances, who will choose further casts when you leave? Will future casting be the responsibility of the artistic director in consultation with the choreographer for the duration of the company's licence to perform the work? Make sure agreements are in writing. An artistic director may suggest casting alternatives for your consideration based on his or her personal knowledge of suitable or developing artists within the company. You are entitled to air any reservations you may have. On the other hand, you might have full confidence in that judgement and endorse the casting proposals.

You may agree that the casting of principals or leading dancers will be by mutual agreement for a specified period, but that the casting of all other parts will be the responsibility of the artistic director and approved assistants who understand the requirements. Whether you wish to be notified of all casting alternatives may depend on the scale of the choreography in question.

If alternative casts are to be taught and rehearsed in your absence, specify who will have this responsibility.

If you know that the commissioning company plans to perform your work for a limited season only, but that a revival of it seems likely within a couple of years, reserve the right to review casting decisions in consultation with the artistic director.

It is advisable to check on the 'local' or contractual interpretation of 'understudy' to avoid any problems (for any particular performer) due to mis-interpretation.

## Children

If your choreography involves children or young people, discuss in advance any opportunities to see their work. Will you visit the school or college, see dance classes, conduct workshops?

If you are not available to select the young people, can your assistant, a member of the company's staff, or a member of the school or college staff do this for you? Does the designated person know exactly what your requirements are?

It is advisable to check on the regulations applicable to the inclusion of children in theatre productions. Take advice from the company manager, children's manager, supervisor or Local Authority Education Department.

Remember to cast understudies, and license them in addition to the principal casts for all necessary rehearsals and performances.

*See also:*
**Child performance regulations** (page 162)

**Working as a choreographer in schools and youth organisations:**
Double casting and understudies (page 88)
Costume (page 90)
Final or stage rehearsal (page 90)
Pre-performance warm-up or rehearsal (page 91)

**Working abroad** (page 103)

## *Guest artists*

It is advisable to check on the company policy with regard to the engagement of guest artists, particularly when an artist is not fully available to you. Although commitment to special performances may have been defined, it is **essential** to check on, or endeavour to secure, his or her attendance at sufficient studio and stage rehearsals and costume fittings. It is also very important to be assured that any guest artist engaged to dance in a new or existing work of yours is suitable, and knows exactly what will be involved in terms of time, energy and commitment.

If the guest artists dance together, check that they will be available to rehearse together for a sufficient number of studio and stage rehearsals.

Try not to agree to the casting of a guest artist whose work you do not know unless the recommendation is extremely detailed and comes from someone whose judgement you trust.

You may require understudies to rehearse in place of guest artists until their arrival.

*See also:*
**Working as a choreographer in opera and musical theatre:**
Non-availability of performers (page 57)

*Availability of performers*
The management must ensure that the cast **is** available to you. If some people are not, temporarily, you might agree to work without them for a limited period. You should be supplied with details of any permitted absences which will affect your rehearsal plans, and understudies for absentees should be informed.

It is important to establish your responsibility towards any second cast. Will you be expected to teach them the work being developed by the first cast each day?

*Animals and birds*
The engagement of trained supervisors, and matters of 'housing', care and safety both on and off stage, are important considerations when working with animals, birds or any other creature. Ask the supervisor about the creature's temperament and involve the cast in any necessary handling techniques. Check on the animal's and supervisor's availability to rehearse and attend stage and technical rehearsals and all performances. Will an alternative 'cast' (!) be necessary? Take specialist advice from Equity on any necessary insurance for creatures and cast. The company will need a special licence to enable it to use animals in both rehearsal and performance.

*See also:*
**Health and safety:**
Special effects or equipment (page 160)

## 5. Audition procedure
Audition procedures vary considerably depending on the choreographer, the commissioning management and the nature and scale of the production.

As yours is a key role, it is advisable to discuss proposals in advance. Equity has negotiated a Code of Conduct for Auditions with the Theatres' National Committee which includes the Theatrical Management Association (TMA), the Society of London Theatre (SOLT) and the Independent Theatre Council (ITC). You are advised to obtain a copy of the code from the Equity office.

*See also:*
**Useful addresses** (booklet)

Consider the following:

✦ If the cast will be an assembly of freelance performers, where will audition notices be placed or published and when?

✦ What information is given on the audition notice?

41

◆ Will the services of a translator be needed at the audition?

◆ Are you aiming at a shortlist followed by a final selection all on one day?

◆ When will performers, understudies and reserve casts be informed of the outcome of the audition? Will this happen by personal contact, telephone or post? Who will notify people?

Choreographers and their assistants have drawn attention to circumstances in which the management has not been prompt in issuing contracts to successful auditionees. Having received no contract, these performers have accepted work and are no longer available.

Remember to select a sufficient number of understudies (though this will probably depend on the production budget) and keep a number of auditionees in reserve in case any member of the cast withdraws whilst under contract. Remember to:

◆ check the dates and times of auditions and any re-call sessions in reserve.

◆ check that your collaborators are also informed and, if necessary, available.

◆ ensure that you have a suitable studio with adequate dimensions and an appropriate surface

◆ check that there will be adequate changing rooms and toilet facilities for both male and female performers, especially if large numbers are anticipated.

◆ ask for an assistant to help you marshal large groups, check names, addresses and telephone numbers, or ask your normal assistant to help you.

◆ alert your assistant if he or she is required to teach class, help with workshops, or demonstrate choreography for you.

◆ check that you will be provided with an accompanist of sufficient skill, and that he or she has all the necessary music in advance (complete with cuts or additions marked) if required to play extracts from a score.

Think through the most effective form of audition. Will you teach a technique class, workshop, improvisation session, or have interviews or one-to-one session with individual performers? Are auditionees expected to sing, dance and/or play a musical instrument? Discuss (with your collaborators if relevant) the audition procedure best suited to your task.

There may be circumstances in which a preliminary (or even final) selection of performers has been made prior to your engagement as choreographer. These performers could be actors who move well or have special skills, or active 'semi-retired' dancers. Try to get basic information about the preliminary selection before your final selection session. In the case of a final selection made before your arrival, it would be advisable to insist on the provision of a session or half-session in which you and the selected performers meet each other. You may want to set movement-work in order to find out how well they move and how they respond to you.

## 6. Travel arrangements

The following list may be useful during you preparation period, whether you are working in Britain or abroad.

✦ Have your travel arrangements been confirmed?

✦ When will you receive all the necessary tickets?

✦ Have you got the necessary bus, coach, train, air, ferry timetables and maps for reference?

✦ Will there be other travel arrangements to be made before you return home?

✦ Do you need to be met? How will you recognise the person meeting you?

✦ If you are going to work abroad, have your travel arrangements left sufficient time for recovery before you start auditions or rehearsals?

If a company proposes a pre-paid air or rail ticket with a specified return date (not open-ended), check in advance that you will be able to see sufficient performances of your work before having to return home. This will be a matter of negotiation between you and the host company as it may entail additional subsistence costs if you stay beyond the first night. Discuss in advance if an open-ended ticket is more suitable for your needs, though you may be responsible for any extra costs.

See also:
**Money:**
Expenses (Travel) (page 14)

**Working abroad** (page 103)

**Contract** (page 3)

# 7. Accommodation arrangements

*I had agreed to a self-contained flat, and asked to be situated close to the station as I had to travel to London at regular intervals to prepare a forthcoming job in Geneva. It seemed almost impertinent to ask the large international company for whom I was working whether anyone had checked the flat's suitability for a month's stay in winter. No-one had. Clearly, I wasn't a 'star'. I arrived at an address which wasn't convenient for rehearsals or the station. Entry to the flat was at the back of the house along an unlit passageway. The flat was bitterly cold, damp and insecure, and when I drew the thin bedroom curtains, fabric and plaster cascaded to the floor. When I sat on the bed a leg broke irreparably. Underneath there were already two bricks in service. After rehearsals the next day I packed and moved onto the pavement to await a taxi.*

Ann Whitley, choreologist.

The following list may be helpful during your preparation period, whether you are working in Britain or abroad:

✦ Will you be able to live at and work from home while under contract? If not, where will you stay?

✦ What sort of accommodation is the company proposing or providing?

✦ What does the accommodation comprise, and will all the facilities as described be suitable?

✦ Are the facilities suitable for an accompanying child, spouse or partner joining you at a later stage ?

✦ If the facilities are self-catering, what equipment does the kitchen/bathroom/lounge contain?

✦ Does the accommodation have a telephone and answering machine, video playback facilities for your use after rehearsals, power sockets for computer, fax and other electrical equipment?

Some companies have difficulty in finding suitable, affordable non-hotel accommodation for guests due to a local shortage. It is important to be satisfied that any accommodation offered to you and paid for by the company (whether it is a hotel, a self-contained apartment or a temporarily vacant house) has been visited, thoroughly checked and approved by someone whose judgement you have reason to trust. A brief printed description of the facilities may hide important defects. It is particularly important to acquire accurate details if your stay is going to last several weeks.

Find out whether the hotel accommodation provided and paid for you also includes breakfast. What does 'breakfast' include?!

*See also:*

**Money:**
Expenses (Accommodation) (page 15)

**Contract** (page 3)

## 8. Administrative tasks

*Personal details*
Some important details may be supplied to the company by your agent. If you are working alone and do not already have the following facts listed and accessible, you may find it useful to prepare some information to give to the host company along with any current biography, photographs and publicity material. Make several copies and add further details as and when necessary:

✦ name, address, telephone and fax number

✦ date and place of birth

✦ nationality (as stated on your passport)

✦ National Insurance number

✦ Schedule D and Income Tax reference number

✦ Value Added Tax (VAT) number if registered

✦ agent or manager's name, address, telephone and fax number

✦ Equity number if relevant

✦ next of kin or solicitor's name, address, telephone and fax number (especially if you are travelling around throughout any period of negotiation or preparation).

It will also be necessary to give bank (name, address, branch code number and account number) and passport (number, date and place of issue, expiry date, names if different from names by which you are known) details to the company.

*Company information*
It may contribute to your own research

and planning to have some printed information about a company or group's artistic policy, history, size and repertory, especially if you are not very familiar with the organisation which is commissioning you. A company's publicity department (where relevant) will rarely have any objection to supplying background information such as a company brochure.

Your integration into company life will be helped if you have a list of the dancers', singers' and actors' names, as well as those of the managerial staff, along with a description of what they do. This information will facilitate your swift access to members of staff you may need to approach about, for instance, rehearsal facilities, schedules, props, subsistence allowance, archives, medical attention or physiotherapy.

### A seat for the first performance

Some managements will attend to all your needs throughout your visit, but it is advisable to check on company or venue policy on the provision of complimentary seats. Do not **assume** that a first night seat will be provided for you, or that you will be able to obtain complimentary seats for your friends or professional contacts. Check that any seat(s) allocated will be situated in a part of the auditorium from which you can see the whole stage or performing area. In some theatres (even some new ones) a side box seat may offer a certain glamour but an incomplete view of the action on stage. It might be wise to ask for seats at the end of a row to provide a speedy escape should it be necessary!

You may want to check on the provision of seats available for you and/ or your assistant throughout a season of performances. If free seats are not available for financial reasons, ask to be shown other authorised sitting or standing areas for your or your assistant's use during performances. It may be necessary to carry your security pass for checking by theatre attendants and security staff.

> *On one of the occasions I'd been working in Holland, I found myself locked into the theatre for a night! I had been invited to do a radio interview about the production I was directing and choreographing. Since the broadcast was going out on various European networks, I'd agreed to respond first in Dutch then in German. To do this I suggested we found somewhere quiet, away from the noise of the stage crew setting up, and the orchestra having its final rehearsal. Off we went to the top of the building. After the interview the whole place seemed deadly quiet. My interviewer and I arrived at stage level to find everyone had gone home, locking up securely behind them. Although we were able to move freely about the building, we had no access to any telephones or food, so there we remained until early morning.*
>
> Michael Holmes, choreographer

### Security pass

Remember to carry with you at all times any necessary identity or security passes which may be given to you to enable you to use main entrances and stage doors, or to allow your free movement within the company's headquarters and the buildings of a theatre complex, including the use of a pass-door between the back stage area and the auditorium or performance space.

## 9. Publicity

A commissioning company should consult you, the choreographer, about the inclusion of your name and the representation of your work in press statements, programmes, souvenir brochures, gala programmes, posters, items of merchandise, or the sleeves of records, discs and videos on sale to the public, in so far as these items are still within the company's control.

A commissioning company should also consult you about the choice of production photographs for press and publicity purposes. Ask if there are deadlines for the choice of these, and for what purpose the photographs will be used.

If you are concerned to build up your own 'archive' of publicity material, ask the press and public relations department to save you some programmes, photographs, press clippings and articles. It is usually possible to arrange for a selection of material to be sent to you some time after the first performance or first season of performances. Make sure your agent or manager also has a copy of this material.

If the commissioning of your choreography, or the music or design for it, for example, has been made possible through a grant or sponsorship arrangement, it would be advisable to ask the commissioning management to inform you of the sum given and whether there are any conditions attached which might affect you.

For example:

✦ Are there any personal or social obligations such as public appearances, 'Friends' events, media interviews or reports to be written?

✦ Are there any creative obligations, advantages, limitations or complications?

✦ Are there any political, social, commercial or geographical considerations?

✦ Are there any time limits for the creation of the choreography, music or design?

It is important to know, when working under contract in the UK or abroad, whether the company has a policy regarding interviews. If you are approached by the media, check first before responding to such requests.

*See also:* **Contract** (page 3)

## 10. Programme credits

### The choreographer and the choreography

If the form and position of your name has not already been agreed in your contract, you should discuss this before the programme publication deadline.

A company press and publications department is likely to ask you for a portrait photograph and biographical details (if these have not already been supplied by your agent). Never be diverted from checking your biography, wherever you work, especially if it is likely to have been edited or translated. Ask to see it in advance of programme compilation deadlines.

If your choreography has been identified by a working title throughout the rehearsal period, establish the final title and inform all relevant departments of the spelling of the words used, as well as any appropriate translation.

Ensure that you supply or approve any synopsis or choreographic background information used, and that you see any additional music or design information which may be included.

*See also:* **Contract** (page 3)

### The cast and other contributors

For the benefit of both press and public, who may be keen to identify particular performers in your work, it is worth considering the assistance offered by a particular programme layout for the names of your cast. This is especially helpful if there is no obvious costume or character-identification in the work, and no easily recognisable order of appearance. The best scheme may only become apparent when your choreography is complete. It is advisable to warn the programme compilers if you intend to devise cast layouts which are other than a straightforward list, since you may be asking for a variation on a standard programme identity.

If your work is dedicated to a mentor, artist or friend, provide or discuss and check the form of wording. Make sure that acknowledgement is made to the author and publisher of any texts or historical information used. It may be necessary to acknowledge permission from the estate of a deceased author. Ask the estate for the correct form of wording.

### The sponsor or funding body

The commissioning company should consult any organisation which sponsors or funds your work about the correct form of wording for their acknowledgement, plus details of any business symbol or logo which should be attached.

### Checklist

Whether it is the responsibility of the commissioning company or yours as director of your own group (devising your own printed programme), various contributions to a production, apart from those of the performers and principal contributors, are entitled to acknowledgement. You may like to use the following checklist for guidance according to your individual circumstances. It is by no means common, however, for all these credits to be made in a company programme:

✦ Name of company
✦ Company's artistic director
✦ Title of work
✦ Date of first performance
✦ Producer/director of production
✦ Choreographer
✦ Other movement specialists
✦ Composer
✦ Conductor/music staff
✦ Title of music or sound source
✦ Authors and publishers of text
✦ Cast
✦ Musicians
✦ Set designer
✦ Costume designer
✦ Lighting designer
✦ Sound designer
✦ Rehearsal director
✦ Rehearsal staff and teachers
✦ Notator or personal assistant
✦ Costume supervisor
✦ Children's supervisor
✦ Technical staff

✦ Stage management
✦ Production staff
✦ Prop maker
✦ Designers of additional millinery, shoes and masks
✦ Venue staff list
✦ Funding bodies
✦ Individual sponsors
✦ Suppliers of free equipment or services
✦ Dedications and personal thanks
✦ Press and public relations
✦ Marketing
✦ Education
✦ Suppliers of machinery or special equipment
✦ Photographers
✦ Film or video-makers
✦ Film or video-operators
✦ Administration and finance
✦ Secretarial staff
✦ Archivist/Librarian
✦ Medical/physiotherapy

If you have limited financial resources, you can produce simple programmes and publicity with a basic desk-top publishing software package. These can then be printed at very low cost.

*See also:*

**Music:** Programme and publicity credits for music (page 127)

## 11. Making a complaint

As a rule, only use a company's formal complaints procedures as a last resort. Most disputes can be solved by discussion, mutual understanding, compromise and tolerance. You would be well advised to have the nature and extent of your complaint clear in your mind, and preferably written down. An informal meeting often resolves a problem. Do not allow a problem to drag on. Try to resolve it at a convenient rehearsal break or at the end of the day. Here is a list of possible problem areas with suggestions as to your first move:

**Is your complaint about the professional job you are trying to do? Refer to:**

✦ your employer, or the producer or director of the production

✦ the company or stage manager

✦ your colleagues in the creative team

✦ the performers with whom you are working

✦ your contract

✦ your agent or manager

✦ your union

✦ your solicitor

**Is your complaint about the premises in which you are working? Refer to:**

✦ the owner or administrator of the premises

✦ the local authority

**Is your complaint about working conditions and/or safety at work? Refer to:**

✦ government or local authority legislation

✦ fire regulations

✦ employment law

**Is your complaint about race, gender or disability discrimination? Refer to:**

✦ Equal Opportunities legislation

✦ the Equal Opportunities policy of the employer

✦ the Race Relations Act

✦ legislation for disabled people

When your problem has been resolved, a note or expression of thanks to someone who has helped to improve the conditions for your work will always be appreciated.

*See also:*
**Health and safety** (page 156)

## 12. Transfers: consultation with the production team

The transfer of a production to a larger theatre does not necessarily bring a larger or similarly-shaped stage. The auditorium may seat more people than the original venue, but your choreography may, in fact, have to be substantially adapted to suit the new performing area and sight-lines. Ask for detailed information, including ground plans, and consider the work which may be involved. Consult the other members of the creative production team such as set and costume designer, lighting designer, composer or musical director, chorus manager and notator-assistant. Your collaborators will have their own enquiries to make, whether the transfer is to be in the UK or abroad.

✦ Will there need to be auditions?

✦ Will you need to look at a new venue and meet production staff?

✦ Will you be undertaking the re-staging work alone, or will you require the assistance of a rehearsal director, notator-repetiteur, assistant and/or previous member of the cast to teach, coach, rehearse, re-stage part or all of the production?

✦ Has the management contacted your approved assistant with a detailed proposal including dates, and is he or she available?

✦ Have you, or has the management, consulted your approved assistant when planning the best use of rehearsal time?

✦ Who will be guardian of the choreography throughout the revival and performance period and on tour?

✦ Who will teach and coach alternative casts?

✦ How many other casts will there be?

Some choreographers' assistants keep rehearsal schedules and notes from previous revivals. These can be very helpful when planning a further revival or transfer. There may be summaries of the time required to teach a section to a certain group, or the time it took to integrate different groups of performers, as well as notes on the number of studios and staff required.

An experienced assistant (where appropriate) may be able to contribute to substantial savings in rehearsal time and costs for the company wanting to revive your work, whilst maintaining the original quality and standards of the production. Alternative casts will also benefit from coaching and polishing by you and/or your assistant.

*See also:*
**Assistants, notators and staff producers** (page 111)

**Money** (page 11)

**Contract** (page 3)

**Copyright** (page 151)

**Working abroad** (page 103)

**Equity** (page 24)

PART 3

# PART 3

## Working as a choreographer

in opera and musical theatre

for a play

for a film

for an advertising commercial

for television: three examples

with schools and youth organisations

in the community

for a specific site or occasion: organisation

Working abroad

# Working as a choreographer in opera and musical theatre

Although some choreographers for opera or musical theatre productions are engaged a year or more in advance, it is not unusual for the engagement of a choreographer to be one of the last decisions to be made concerning the creative production team—often long after the appointment of the set and costume designer(s) and lighting designer. It is likely that important musical and design decisions will have been made a year or more before your appointment. In this environment, you then face a very particular kind of collaboration, and the challenge of finding a skilful way to integrate choreography into a prescribed context.

1. What are you contracted to undertake?

2. Other choreographers or movement specialists

3. The creative hierarchy

4. Dates and times

5. Rehearsal sessions

6. Non-availability of performers

7. Printed rehearsal schedules

8. Company personnel lists

9. Cast lists

10. Programme credit

11. Actors, singers and 'non-dancers'

12. Microphones

13. Surtitles

14. Pre-performance warm-up or rehearsal

15. Post-production care

The advice in this chapter is also relevant to choreographers working in **plays, operetta, pantomime, revue, 'period' dance productions,** and some is also applicable to those working in **film** or **television**. For more specific information on choreography within a play, film or TV, see relevant chapters in this guide.

There is at the moment no standard Equity agreement for choreographers working in opera. It is advisable to ask your agent to handle the contract from an opera company. If you do not have an agent, consult the Money, Music and Contract sections of this guide.

A note on terminology: in the UK the person who directs an opera production is sometimes known as 'the producer' rather than 'the director'.

## 1. What are you contracted to undertake?

Find out exactly what kind of choreography, movement or staging is required, where the choreography occurs in the production and in the music score, its purpose or context, and for how many minutes, hours or scenes it is needed. You may want to ask some of the following questions:

✦ Is there a need for dances for professional dancers with a specific training or for dancers with a broad experience in a wide variety of dance forms and styles?

✦ Will dances of a particular historical period be required? If so, which period and which country of origin?

✦ Will these dances be performed by dancers, singers, actors, children or a combination of performers?

✦ Will you be required to help individual singers and actors move in a particular style while negotiating a hazardous set and complicated text?

✦ Are you required to provide dramatic action to delineate a particular character or general movement ideas in collaboration with the director or producer?

✦ Is your role to act as a bridge between producer, musical director and actors?

✦ Does the producer read music?

✦ Will you be responsible for the musical staging of the production? Does this mean all action that is staged to musical accompaniment or specific scenes with specific performers?

You may find you have to provide 'instant choreography' and ideas during rehearsals while also responding to staging problems and challenges.

You and the producer/director must have sufficient time to discuss all aspects of your creative contribution. Ideally, this should happen well in advance of any time you wish to allocate for historical research or musical preparation. There will be very little time during the rehearsal period in which to address and resolve areas of misunderstanding. If there is an aspect of staging or choreography which you both agree to leave undefined during your preliminary discussions, it will be important to ensure that you and the producer/director see enough of each other's separate work during the rehearsal period to keep in touch with the development of each other's ideas. This will enable you to leave unresolved staging decisions until a late point in the knowledge that you are both 'thinking in the same way'.

## 2. Other choreographers or movement specialists

Ask if there will be other choreographers working on the production. These might be experts in:

+ Tap dance

+ Jazz dance

+ Folk dance

+ Martial arts

+ Western 'historical', social or court dance

+ 'Historical' dance from other cultures

+ Kathak or Bharata Natyam

+ Special effects

+ Acrobatics or circus skills

+ Fight arrangement/direction

Arrange to meet any of these specialist collaborators. Discuss your individual approach to the work, your areas of responsibility within the production, and how other specialists' work will affect yours. What collaboration is possible between you and another movement specialist given the practical constraints of the production? If you can foresee problems, are they acceptable under the circumstances?

Ask the producer/director if the cast, production staff and stage management understand (at least in principle) the proposed contribution of all choreographers involved.

If the production company is a member of the Society of London Theatre or the Theatrical Management Association, and is thus employing staff on either Equity/SOLT or Equity/TMA West End Agreements, then it will have entered an agreement to use a fight director rather than a choreographer to stage any fights.

## 3. The creative hierarchy

While acknowledging the position of the conductor at the top of the production hierarchy of opera and other musical productions, it is important to know any hierarchical structure existing among the choreographers or movement specialists engaged, and how it is anticipated that this hierarchy will work. If you know the other choreographers or movement specialists involved, it may be obvious to you that one of them is considered the senior by virtue of experience or specialism. With or without an order of 'importance', the inclusion of several choreographers will require from the management and producer/director a skilled and flexible approach to rehearsal spaces, scheduling and staging time.

*See also:* **Music: Working with conductors or musical directors (page 125)**

## 4. Dates and times

You should be provided with some of the following information, but if you have not:

+ Find out when your rehearsals are due to begin and how much time you have in which to choreograph.

+ Find out when the conductor will be present if not available from the first rehearsals onwards. If relevant, find out who is the conductor's deputy.

+ If you are going to choreograph a work for a singing or acting chorus, is the time allocated sufficient? Is there a block of consecutive rehearsals devoted to dance and stylised movement, or is there a limited number of chorus rehearsals through several weeks?

✦ Find out the starting date for dancers', actors' and singers' contracts.

✦ Find out when full production rehearsals begin if different from those mentioned above.

✦ Although it should be stated in your contract, check the date and time of the first performances, any previews, and all subsequent performances (as far as is known) and any tours.

✦ Ask for the date of the general or dress rehearsal. Ask if it will be open to the public or a 'Friends' audience — though this is a decision that may not be made until a few days beforehand.

✦ Ask at which rehearsals press photographers may be present.

✦ Ask for a schedule of technical and lighting rehearsals, piano-stage rehearsals and full orchestra, band or ensemble rehearsals. Ask which of these will be in partial or full costume, including wigs and make-up.

✦ Find out at which rehearsals the chorus can be present, and for how long.

✦ Find out at which studio rehearsals any special floor coverings, flooring, rostra, ramps, furniture or sections of set will be available, and when any or all of them will be transferred to the stage and assembled securely for stage rehearsals.

If there does not appear to be a session allocated to the choreographer for his or her own placing or polishing call on stage with musical accompaniment, insist that there is an adjustment made to the schedule as early as possible to accommodate your needs (even if half of a three hour session is all that is available). Remember that you will be expected to have set all your choreography before the production moves from rehearsal studio to stage or performance area.

If you are new to choreography within opera and musical theatre, you will now realise that a production schedule has often been planned or fixed months or years in advance. You are entering a complex financial, technical and artistic structure involving many people in different areas of work. You may have been unable to contribute to the construction of the advance schedule, but are expected to work efficiently within it. If you need to make a change in the schedule, it must be proposed at the earliest possible opportunity as any alteration is likely to have repercussions in several departments and may be difficult to accommodate.

*See also:*
**Child performance regulations**
(page 162)

## 5. Rehearsal sessions

*By sheer chance you hear someone say to the wardrobe staff (and the choreographer hasn't been consulted); 'of course you can do costume fittings between 2pm and 3.30pm—it's only a dance call'. The implication is that, irrespective of which combination of performers is involved, dance is the constituent part of the production which can easily be interrupted and deprived of its rehearsal time...*

Stuart Hopps, choreographer

Rehearsals are normally divided into morning, afternoon, evening and weekend sessions. Performers may be called in separate groupings—for instance, principal singers, chorus, actors, dancers, children or in various combinations.

It is important to understand how long each session can be, the maximum number of sessions which can be worked in a day and in a week, and any limitation posed by individual or group availability. Some artists and staff may not be exclusively available to you because they are rehearsing or performing in a simultaneous production. This usually occurs when working with a company which operates a repertory system, where activities are based on a number of different productions with overlapping rehearsal and performance periods. Pay particular attention to the availability of principal singers and any special guests with whom you will be working, especially if you know they have a busy personal schedule which involves travelling to engagements abroad. Check with the management that the artists in question are aware of what may be involved choreographically when their schedule requires their attendance at your rehearsals.

Find out about the patterns of statutory rest and meal breaks throughout the working day. Note that a three hour session with a twenty minute break leaves you with only two and a half hours **productive** rehearsal time.

Find out if there are any limitations on the amount of time in rehearsal sessions during which a chorus can dance. In some companies this may be limited to half of a three hour call.

## 6. Non-availability of performers

The complexity and variety of international casting systems means that some managements may not consult the choreographer about, or provide a list of, some of the performer's agreed absences from specified rehearsals or performances (marked on rehearsal schedules as 'n/a's'). Ask to be informed at the earliest opportunity to enable you to plan effective rehearsals and cope with missing artists. Check that understudies ('covers') will attend where possible.

You will meet a variety of responses from companies (and other choreographers) to artists' requests for absence. Some managements have a firm but sympathetic attitude to the status of freelance artists who may have a previous professional engagement or audition which interrupts their commitment to 'your' schedule.

## 7. Printed rehearsal schedules

Each performing arts organisation has its own design and layout for the daily, weekly or advance schedule. If your rehearsal requirements have been translated into the language of a company schedule (in the UK or abroad), check that you understand how to interpret the information, including the abbreviations, initials and code numbers. You will also want to check that all your rehearsals and cast's fittings are listed. A company operating a repertory system is likely to have an extensive and densely printed schedule listing many different productions and with many different studios and personnel included.

*See also:*
**Working as a choreographer:**
Rehearsals (Schedules) (page 34)

## 8. Company personnel lists

To help integration into a company and production, ask to be provided with a company personnel list. You may need to know exactly how the music department functions, who the chorus manager is and how he can help you. You will want to know which member of the stage management team will be 'on the book' or 'calling the show'. You will want to know the right department and person to approach about, for instance, money, rehearsal schedules and medical attention.

## 9. Cast lists

If not already provided for you, ask for complete cast lists (singers, actors, dancers, children and other performers) and check to see whether the chorus listing has divided the members of the chorus into soprano, mezzo soprano, tenor and bass. These divisions and any sub-divisions may affect the stage groupings with which you will be able to work.

*See also:*
**Working as a choreographer:**
Casting (page 39)

## 10. Programme credit

Although you may have been identified as 'the choreographer' throughout the rehearsal period of a production, many choreographers and choreographer-directors are very particular about the words used to acknowledge their creative contribution. This is a legitimate concern if the amount of choreography and staging included in the production is greater than first estimated, or if the role of the choreographer has altered during the rehearsal period. Discuss your programme credit with your agent as well as with the publicity, publications or administration staff in advance of programme compilation deadlines. Other forms of acknowledgement could be:

✦ Movement Director:

✦ Movement by...

✦ Movement and staging by...

✦ Musical staging and choreography by...

✦ Direction and choreography by...

✦ Co-director and choreographer:

*See also:*
**Working as a choreographer:**
Programme credits (page 46)

## 11. Actors, singers and non-dancers

The expression 'non-dancer' is often used to define a range of people extending from those who may have been professional dancers to those who may be singers or actors with minimal but valuable dance or movement training, all of whom have been engaged to learn stylised forms of movement or dance. It is necessary to be sensitive to an actor or singer's pace of learning, one which will be very different from that of a trained dancer. Confidence and skill may take time to nurture, especially if a combination of acting, singing and dancing is required. Some of your original ideas will need to be refined. Many will be reduced to the minimum effective moves with which the performers feel confident.

Be aware that much of what you devise or choreograph for singers, whether principals or chorus groupings, may be conditioned by their need to see the conductor or a television monitor, and by their need to project their voices into the auditorium.

It is advisable to recommend that non-dancers, singers and actors who have agreed to 'dance' or move expansively (including kneeling or lying down) attend rehearsals in suitably comfortable or protective clothing and footwear. If you have specific clothing recommendations these could be helpful to the performers. Find out whether this advice should come from you or a member of the management team, and make sure it is given in advance of the first rehearsal.

In opera each member of the cast is expected to arrive at the first rehearsal knowing his or her own music and text very well. The first rehearsals for a musical or a play, however, are often devoted to learning songs and script. You may have to begin to choreograph or stage movement while the cast still has 'the book' in hand.

Although not primarily your responsibility, it might in some circumstances be advisable to check with the opera or theatre management that the contract of freelance dancers and any other performers who 'dance' gives them enough time to warm up and apply any necessary costume or make-up before early morning stage rehearsals.

## 12. Use of microphones

If microphones (mics) are going to be placed on stage, find out exactly where they will be located so that you can choreograph movement and staging which does not disturb them. Sometimes directional mics are placed along the front of the stage.

If you are choreographing performers whose voices will be amplified while they dance or 'move', you will need to know what sort of mic they will be given. It could be:

✦ a clip-on radio mic with transmitter

✦ a hand-held radio mic (no cable)

✦ a hand-held, hard-wired mic (with cable attached)

Some radio mics may need special licences from the suppliers.

Some of your choreographic considerations could concern:

✦ the length of any cable and what to do with it

✦ advice on microphone handling technique

✦ the placing of clip-on mics and pocket transmitters

In these cases, you may want to consult the sound engineer and/or designer or wardrobe supervisor. Mics can be attached to the front of a wig, the front of a costume or a jacket lapel. A transmitter could be attached to the body in a variety of places depending on the garments worn.

## 13. Surtitles

If the production in which your choreography appears is one in which surtitles (or 'supertitles') are provided above the stage action to help the audience understand the libretto and plot, try to find time to watch them during a rehearsal, or ask for a copy of the surtitle script from the script-writer. You and the producer might want to check that the dramatic action directly relates to the limited portions of surtitle text used at any particular moment. Choreographers have sometimes noticed (too late to suggest any alteration) that the surtitle translation of a phrase in the plot has been literal or direct, whereas the dramatic action has required a colloquial or ironic translation (or vice versa).

## 14. Pre-performance warm-up or rehearsal

Pre-performance classes and warm-ups will almost certainly be scheduled by dance company managements. If you work in musical theatre, opera or plays, however, in which dancers, singers or actors dance, you may have to explain to that management the need for the provision of a physical and/or musical warm-up or run-through of certain sections of choreography prior to the first and possibly all subsequent performances.

In opera, there could be as much as three of four days 'rest' for singers' voices between the final stage rehearsal and the first performance. There may also be technical and repertory programming reasons for this period without further rehearsal. Dancers, however, need to keep fit. Company or union regulations, and the sheer inconvenience for many departments and performers (without advance warning) make it virtually impossible to schedule a pre-performance run-through **at the last minute,** except in the case of a genuine emergency. However, if the need for a limited warm-up or run-through is explained and discussed in advance, along with the artistic benefits to be derived, with health and safety factors acknowledged, some managements may be able to negotiate and schedule some form of warm-up time. You may need to press hard, and success may be limited to a run-through with just one group or one rank of performer.

Care and diplomacy is required to balance your legitimate desire for your work always to be seen at its best— avoiding any gradual deterioration through lack of rehearsal or 'refreshment'—with the management's mass of practical considerations such as financial, union, rehearsal space and timetabling matters.

Remember that a pre-performance warm-up may need musical accompaniment, music staff, and a member of staff to supervise it. The best time for a run-through may mean that it is not possible to hold it on stage because the performance space is required by the technical and production staff prior to a performance. Another adequate space with the right facilities must be found.

## 15. Post-production care

Check your contract to see what is required with regard to any scheduled visits to your production during a season of performances or while the production is on tour. Attendance of this kind may be necessary to monitor standards of performance, to see other casts, or to launch alternative casts. This work could be done in association with your assistant, subject to contractual arrangements. Check the dates of visits if specified, and the agreed travel, accommodation and subsistence allowances, as well as the provision of a seat to see the performance. Make sure you have a tour schedule.

*See also:*

**Assistants, notators and staff producers** (page 111)

**Contract** (page 3)

**Money** (page 11)

**Music** (page 120)

**Working as a choreographer** (page 31)

**Working abroad** (page 103)

# Working as a choreographer for a play

This chapter has been written in association with <u>Working as a choreographer in opera and musical theatre</u> and <u>Music</u>. It is therefore very important to read all three chapters in conjunction, since many relevant subjects are not repeated here.

1.  What are you contracted to undertake?

2.  Your contract

3.  Royalties

4.  Rehearsals

5.  Rehearsal assistants and dance captains

6.  Re-casting and touring

## 1. What are you contracted to undertake?

When approached by a producer, production company, national company or regional theatre to choreograph a play, find out who the author is and who the director will be. Ask for the script and organise a meeting with the director (and author, if it is a new play). Will you be able to work together effectively? What are your ideas?

It is important to know the script very well, and it might be an advantage to know other works by the same author. Try to get copies of all necessary music, tapes, scores which may form part of the production. Arrange a meeting with the composer or arranger, conductor or musical director and accompanist.

Try to discover as much as possible about the nature and expectation of your collaboration, as this will directly affect your contract and agreement. You may be engaged as a specialist to provide a social dance from another century to conclude one scene. Alternatively it may be anticipated that your role will be choreographer and assistant director to the whole production. Or, you may be required, as movement director, to provide ideas, assorted choreography and musical staging, character definition and an overall atmosphere and consistent body language for the production. Find out how much of your time will be involved. On occasions, you may foresee the work taking longer than estimated by the director. Explain exactly why this will be so.

Ask to see a model of the set or any available costume and set design. Try to get a ground plan and photographs or copies of designs to keep for reference and ideas.

## 2. Your contract

There are two equity agreements which you may encounter when choreographing for a play:

### The Equity/TMA Agreement

The Equity/Theatrical Management Association Agreement covers the subsidised repertory theatres and commercial non-West End producers. The minimum fee in this agreement covers up to two weeks' rehearsal and three days' pre-production, auditioning and casting. If your rehearsal period extends beyond this period, you will be entitled to a weekly payment in addition to the basic fee for each week or part-week. Additional days of pre- or post-production work attract a daily rate.

A small amount of choreography can be covered by a daily engagement fee— for a maximum of six days (not necessarily consecutive). If you think that you will need more time to complete the job, you should negotiate a fee on the basis of the three-part structure above.

If you are offered an 'all-in' fee, you should analyse it by assessing the length of the rehearsal period, the amount of pre-production required and the extent of post-production work. Ask Equity for current minimum rates. Remember that subsidised theatre employers are assigned to one of four categories, which will be reflected in the minimum fees specified in the Equity/TMA Agreement.

Commercial producers are categorised in a similar way to reflect the distinctions between a major tour or season and a smaller one, and whether the employer is a commercial repertory producer. Check with Equity if you need advice.

You are also entitled to expenses or subsistence as appropriate.

### Equity/SOLT Agreement

If you are working in the West End, you should be engaged on the terms of the Equity/Society of London Theatre Agreement for West End Theatre Choreographers.

Three categories of engagement exist:

✦ choreography/staging for a major musical

✦ choreography/staging for a play

✦ a small amount of choreography/ staging

The first two have minimum fees to cover specified periods of time, with supplementary payments for additional work. The third category provides for a session-based arrangement with a minimum guarantee of four sessions which must include the technical and dress rehearsals and two performances. It follows that you will need a minimum of five sessions under this agreement.

If you are not engaged by a TMA or SOLT member, you could use the structures above as a basis for negotiating a fee. If you need to know other Equity rates (for example, those used by members of the Independent Theatre Council) get in touch with Equity.

*See also:* **Equity** (page 24)

## 3. Royalties

No royalties are paid to choreographers (or directors, writers or many other members of the creative team) in subsidised repertory theatre.

However, in commercial provincial theatre you will be entitled to a royalty. This can be expressed as a fixed negotiated sum per performance but not less than 1% of the initial fee or of the minimum fee prevailing at the time of the performance. You should note here that 'initial fee' means the basic fee for two weeks rehearsal plus any additional weeks' payment. For example, your initial fee for a play with a four week rehearsal period would be made up of the basic fee plus two weeks at the additional weekly rate. Check this carefully when negotiating your royalty.

In the West End—by definition a group of commercial theatres—you are entitled to royalties. These can be expressed in a number of ways:

✦ as a weekly fee (minimums specified in the Equity/SOLT Agreement)

✦ as a percentage of gross box office receipts

✦ as a re-negotiated fee per performance (which must be no less than the sum charged for the highest priced seat in the house for the production)

In certain circumstances—for example if the production runs into serious financial difficulties—you may be asked to waive your royalty if it is above the Equity weekly minimum. Other members of the production team must also be asked to reduce their royalty, and all must be reduced by the same ratio. In any event, you cannot be asked to reduce your royalty below the minimum Equity weekly rate.

If you are engaged on a session-basis only, the Equity Agreement states that a royalty can be negotiated 'where appropriate'.

*See also:* **Money:**
Royalties and residuals (page 12)

## 4. Rehearsals

Musical staging for plays is a very specialised activity. There are some plays in which a choreographer is needed on a constant basis. A play will normally have four weeks' rehearsal whilst a larger musical production may have six weeks'.

In discussion with the producer of the play, you will have agreed which days you will attend during a four week rehearsal period. If your role grows, you must re-negotiate your agreement with the management (or, if circumstances make it inevitable, decline the extra work). This type of re-negotiation is not unusual, though it will require the producer to acknowledge your changing status. The producer should trust your judgement, along with that of the play's director, if he or she wants the best possible result.

It is wise to sit in on rehearsals and meet the actors before your scheduled rehearsals begin, even if the amount of choreography required is very small. The scene will almost certainly have been 'blocked' (the main moves and structure sketched out) before you arrive, so it is advisable to observe how the director has begun to shape the play.

Working on a play means that you may spend a lot of time 'relaxing' and building the confidence of a group of actors, some of whom may consider themselves incapable of 'dancing' and may voice their reservations about the prospect.

It is very important to establish what the actors will be wearing and carrying. Pay particular attention to hats, jewellery, footwear, armoury, and any details of period costume. These details will affect what you can do in the available space.

Working on a play will require a far more flexible attitude to your own choreographic material than when choreographing a work for a dance company. It is wise not to be too 'precious' about the exact nature of your work. You should see it as part of the overall vision of the production.

On stage the demands of other contributors will probably take priority. It is often the case that it is more important to the play to achieve fluent set or lighting changes than an absolutely straight line of actors ready for a dance. As the choreographer, therefore, you will need to be very thorough in the rehearsal room. If the cast are well-rehearsed they will be able to cope with the inevitable technical and artistic alterations which can occur at the last minute without prejudice to specially-choreographed moves or scenes. It is important to remain objective and adaptable.

## 5. Rehearsal assistants and dance captains

If the production team includes an assistant director, he or she will be responsible for the care of your work if, for example, you have choreographed a short dance for one act. Between rehearsals and during a season of performances, if there is no assistant director, you may decide to entrust the responsibility of maintaining the spirit and standard of your work to a particular actor. In this case, be aware of the fact that you may place that actor in a position where he or she expects payment for extra work.

There are seldom rehearsal assistants or dance captains in plays in either the commercial or subsidised theatre, except in large West End shows. If there are, it is usually the choreographer who selects the member of the cast who performs this function.

## 6. Re-casting and touring

When a play is re-cast, it is very unlikely that new actors will interpret your choreography in exactly the same way as the original cast. You may have to accept that, in plays, precision of footwork, for example, is less important than in other dance contexts.

You may be asked to re-stage the original choreography if the production is going on a tour. You may need to alter your staging to accommodate thrust and proscenium stages. This work may not have been mentioned in your original contract but there should be a post-production clause which states that you will agree to return to re-work your choreography for a tour with payment at a daily rate.

If you are working in the subsidised theatre and are required to visit your choreography once a week during the show's season, then you must be paid for these extra hours. If you are in receipt of royalties from a commercial show you will not be paid for this work and will be expected to attend the theatre on a specified number of occasions. This arrangement will be outlined in your contract.

*See also:*

**Working as a choreographer in opera and musical theatre** (page 53)

**Music** (page 120)

**Set and costume design** (page 130)

**Lighting design** (page 136)

**Assistants, notators and staff producers** (page 111)

**Working as a choreographer** (page 31)

**Contract** (page 3)

**Money** (page 11)

**Child performance regulations** (page 162)

# Working as a choreographer for a film

If you are regularly involved in choreographing for films your work may range from the provision of a dance for a leading actor to suit a specific historical period, to the arrangement of the over-all movement 'surround' for scenes which include a wide variety of dancers, actors or 'stars'. This chapter aims to give general advice that will apply to your role, whatever your choreographic responsibilities. It is founded on the approach of various choreographers who work on films for either general release or television broadcast.

1.  Choice of choreographer

2.  Discussions with the director

3.  Negotiation, contract and fee

4.  Casting and auditions

5.  Working with the cast

6.  Preparation

7.  The choreographic process

8.  Design

9.  Music

> *If someone asked me what I would most desire on a film set, I wouldn't ask for an office or a fridge with iced drinks, I'd ask for a quiet place—a room of my own to which I could retreat and think.*
>
> Eleanor Fazan, choreographer

## 1. Choice of choreographer

The director (in this medium the person who directs the film) chooses who he or she wants to provide choreography for the film in question. This selection could be made from a list of names supplied by the producer, it may be as a result of the director's previous partnership with a choreographer in film work, or the choice may be made on the basis of a choreographer's particular reputation.

## 2. Discussions with the director

For some directors 'choreography' remains a mystery. As part of preliminary discussions, you may find it necessary to introduce a director to the nature of the task and its processes. Point out your own fields of work or areas of specialisation. It is important to explain what you see as your strengths—characterisation and motivation for example, or historical dance and drama, individual dance techniques and forms, specially-devised stylised dance or massed movement and staging. This kind of discussion could help a director decide which aspects of choreography and/or more general movement should be your responsibility and which could be jointly handled or devised.

Unless engaged as co-director, a choreographer works 'under' a director.

It is very important to understand a director's 'vision' of the film and how he or she sees your participation or collaboration fitting within it. If not already provided for you, ask for a copy of the screenplay and any other relevant text or literary material.

## 3. Negotiation, contract and fee

Before deciding if you want to accept an invitation to work on a film, and before signing the contract, you will probably be involved in some unpaid meetings. Your inclusion in these will help you find out more about the production, and may provide some indication or specific details of any research that will be necessary. This information could affect the nature of your forthcoming contract. If you feel you are being called to an unreasonable number of meetings, ask to be paid for some of them or, if you sign a contract, make sure that any agreement for fees for this extra work is written into it.

Many choreographers have found that they have not been able to have extensive discussion and the opportunity for contact with the director, as well as time for information-gathering, because they have been engaged by a film company at a very late stage in the production schedule. These are challenging circumstances in which the choreographer has to work fast with little or no time for preparation.

It is advisable to wait until your contract is settled and signed before embarking upon any necessary research.

There is a reference to choreographers in Equity's <u>Cinema Films Agreement</u> which is currently being developed and extended. Contact Equity for details.

Your fee, if based on the Equity daily

rate for choreographers, will be calculated according to the number of shooting days on which your choreography is used. That fee will be guaranteed. If, in fact, you work fewer days than stated the fee will remain as originally calculated. The number of days allocated to shoots may be drawn out over a period of time and you may find you have long gaps between the shoots which include your work. Extra days, perhaps required for musical, literary or visual research, will also be paid at a daily rate. Payment of extra days will depend on the nature and scale of the film, the size of the production company and its budget.

*See also:* **Equity** (page 24)

Attention has been drawn to the often inadequate amount of rehearsal time allocated by the film company for the choreographer to work with members of the cast, whether leading actors or groups of actors and dancers. The production budget often appears not to include provision for any experimentation, coaching or rehearsal. There will be occasions when you should insist on this provision and payment for it. In addition, specify in detail your rehearsal facility requirements, or investigate in advance the suitability of halls or studios recommended for your use. A film company might be sympathetic to your insistence that some rehearsal will contribute to a better film, but the minimum time and cost will be allowed. (Choreographers working on a filmed musical are usually given more rehearsal time).

*See also:* **Working as a choreographer:** Rehearsals (Facilities) (page 35)

A shooting session is of unlimited duration (unlike a rehearsal session in live theatre or dance work). There is no overtime pay and there are no royalties.

It is unusual for a choreographer to be involved in the editing process of, for example, a feature film or film of a play for television. If you have a long and close working relationship with the director, you may be invited to observe and/or contribute. However, it is worth approaching the subject of editing during contractual negotiations. Secure the agreement in your contract.

Try to find out as soon as possible whether the film will be shot on location or in a film studio, or both, and what provision will be made for your accommodation. If you are offered a hotel or apartment, check that it will be adequate for your needs by asking what the accommodation comprises.

*See also:* **Working as a choreographer:** Accommodation arrangements (page 43)

## 4. Casting and auditions

In film, 'stars' are contracted first, then smaller-part actors, with 'extras', dancers and the choreographer often chosen at the last minute. To save money, dancers are often contracted for a very few days prior to the shoot.

If the casting of dancers is by contract your responsibility, find out the maximum number you can select, and discuss the necessary audition or casting procedures. Also find out what assistance is available to you for this process if you are not able to have a full time assistant.

If the choice of dancers or actors has been made prior to your engagement, try to ensure that you have a chance to meet those chosen, particularly 'non-dancers' or extras. If you cannot meet them, try to see their work on video before rehearsals or shooting begins. Leading actors may not be available for you to meet at this stage.

*See also:*
**Working as a choreographer:**
Casting (page 39)
Audition procedure (page 41)

**Working as a choreographer for an advertising commercial:**
Performers, auditions, assistants and rehearsals (page 76)

## 5. Working with the cast

The quality of dancing and the degree of physical expertise among actors will be variable. Your choreographic ideas are likely to be directly affected by both the time available to rehearse and by the ability of a single actor or group of extras. Some may be experienced and skilled but others may have reservations about any kind of 'dancing' and may need extra coaching or encouragement (though this will always be in snatched moments in a tight schedule). Even with limited time, this extra attention may bring the actor confidence which you can then utilise. On the other hand, in a scene which requires a high degree of physical expertise, an actor without the necessary confidence and skill for dancing may be better deployed on the 'sidelines' where his or her presence may have alternative value.

It could be said that part of your success as a choreographer in film work relies on, or results from, an ability to make actors, dancers or singers 'look good' on the screen. On shooting days much of your time may be devoted to

encouraging the actors, dancers and extras. They may need to be reassured of the importance of their presence, however small their role. You may need to be as much a motivator as a deviser of movement and staging.

> *You often have to provide 'instant choreography' with little or no time to research the context. On one occasion I was brought in at the very last minute as choreographer for a scene in a big film. The Italian director needed someone to devise a dance in a French romantic ballet style for a ten year-old French girl. The girl and the dance were required to charm an audience of by-standers and the action was supposed to weave amongst furniture and rugs. The girl was willing and hard-working but spoke little English, had no dance training, no experience of 'turn-out' from the hips, and no experience of remembering dance steps or music. The film company expected the child and me to accomplish everything spontaneously on the set one morning!*
>
> Caroline Pope, choreographer

## 6. Preparation

Apart from research or preparation directly linked to your proposed choreographic work, it would be an advantage to ask the film company for its production and technical personnel list, including people in the company's administration with whom you may need to communicate. This information will help you to understand the production hierarchy and facilitate your work within it.

*See also:*
**Working as a choreographer:**
Administrative tasks (Company information) (page 44)

**Working as a choreographer for an advertising commercial:**
The production team (page 76)

Make sure that you have been provided with rehearsal and shooting schedules and a complete cast 'breakdown' which includes dancers, actors who dance, and extras.

It will be important to plan your mode of transport to guarantee punctuality at the location site for early morning calls and your return home after long, late days. If possible, try to establish in your contract that a film company car will provide you with transport.

It is advisable to carry a tape recorder or CD player, sufficient leads, cables and spare batteries. With copies of the recorded music or text, not only do you have your own portable source of reference, but you can snatch moments of rehearsal with your cast between 'takes' or in a lighting break.

*See also:* **Working as a choreographer:** Rehearsals (Personal equipment) (page 37)

The film company will provide catering at the studio and on location, but if you have special dietary needs, make enquiries in case you need to provide your own food or supplements.

## 7. The choreographic process

You will be required on set on all days

on which your choreography is involved. Your schedule will be dictated by the hours and days when dancers, actors, extras and 'stars' are called. Time will rule your work and, in film, 'time is money'.

It is important to work out, or to be told by the director, the pace of a scene which you are choreographing or in which your choreography appears. Check whether this pace might change.

Usually, you will be involved in choreographing the 'surround' first (the surrounding activity which contributes to the mood, pace, quality or special nature of the scene). The 'stars' or leading actors will be brought into this setting later. Their availability is likely to be limited, since the production company will save money if their involvement on the set is pared down to the minimum. This inevitably means that, if part of your job is to work with a leading actor, time will be very short. Most actors will recognise and respond well to thorough preparation, so it is important to have done your research and to be ready with alternative choreographic options if your first plan does not work or is not liked. There will be no time to withdraw and re-think.

Twenty seconds on film is a 'long' time. The way you choreograph will be affected by the exact timing of the scenes and your sense of time in this medium — time as seconds and minutes and time as movement speed. The camera will 'miss' movement which is too 'fast' (unless the shot is deliberately designed to catch a blurred image), yet there is a pace which, in film, is too 'slow'. Be aware of the power on camera of a slight turn of the head or a glance of the eyes. Ask how much of what you devise will be shot in close-up, and how close this will be. If the whole body is shown, will the feet be visible?

You may not always know which camera angle, tracks and lenses will be used, nor how the shot is being planned, but directors often use monitors on set to view their work. If you study what has just been shot you can sometimes make quick changes or add detail before the next shot.

Sometimes you do not know exactly how long the shot within a certain scene will last. On these occasions it may be necessary and useful to devise a short sequence of movement which is quickly learned and can be successfully repeated several times. With this, an actor or a mixed group of actors and dancers, will perform choreographed material which looks appropriate and 'interesting' irrespective of the angle, distance or duration of the shot.

It often happens that, despite your sensitive shaping of a scene or a shot, the director 'sees' and wants to use your work in a very different way or in a different sequence. The material you consider to be 'best' could end up on the cutting room floor.

## 8. Design

As the choice of choreographer to work on a film is a decision often made long after the choice of designer(s), almost all aspects of design are determined before the choreographer arrives on set. It is advisable, therefore, to try and make an appointment to meet the designers — particularly the costume designer. Ask to see the set and find out about the floor surface, floor levels and any raked staging and stairways. Ask to see the costumes-in-progress and find out in advance what restrictions or enhance-

ment the costume design may place on choreography and cast. Ask about (and if possible see) footwear and props. Although some discussion — and slight accommodation — may be possible with regard to your requirements at this stage, you will usually have to work around the designer's wishes. The 'look' is prioritised on film. Any alterations at a later stage which delay the production team's tight schedule will not be viewed favourably.

*See also:*

**Set and costume design:**
Costume considerations (page 133)
Footwear (page 135)

## 9. Music

Choreographers have drawn attention to a variety of challenges with regard to the use of music in film and its final relationship to any dance or stylised movement.

It is important to try to find out about — or to sense the importance placed on — music by the director, though these discussions may often take place through a second or third assistant director. It is helpful if you can discover whether the music will be used to provide 'atmosphere' or whether, perhaps, live musicians will play and 'act' in a scene with which you are involved.

Choreographers engaged at short notice may only be provided with a recording of 'the music' the day before the shoot. The speed of the version chosen by the director and/or musical director for the shoot may be strikingly different from the version, or versions, you were given for swift preparation and rehearsal. Changes in rhythm and speed will affect your choreography, and possibly its suitability in the required context. It may be necessary to make immediate choreographic adaptations. In this instance, you can rely on trained dancers to make this adjustment fast and without prejudice to your choreographic intentions, but 'untrained' dancers or children may have difficulties which could reflect on the quality and impact of your choreography.

There appear to be fewer problems when a choreographer is asked to choreograph to a commissioned score or commissioned arrangement of existing music. These are circumstances in which the choreographer knows that the music provided, or being written or arranged, will be a component of the final film.

Sometimes a scene in which your choreography appears is shot in silence and any 'music' dubbed later. On occasions it may be possible to assist the cast by standing in the background and, with the aid of headphones and your own recording, to 'conduct' the music for the cast from a position from which dancers can catch your beat.

It is not unusual for a choreographer to be asked to find his or her 'own' music. Some indication of an appropriate composer, century, geographical location, nature and quality of music may be given. However, there appears to be no guarantee that the music you research and choose to work with will be included in the final film.

The cutting and editing process will inevitably affect your work. The sequence of scenes is often changed, and alternative music may be dubbed over choreography specifically devised to, for example, observe historical accuracy.

*See also:*

**Contract** (page 3)

**Money** (page 11)

**Working as a choreographer for a play** (page 62)

**Assistants, notators and staff producers** (page 111)

**Music** (page 120)

# Working as a choreographer for an advertising commercial

The world of advertising often demands a far faster creative process than other media, with advertisement directors and advertising agencies reliant on a great deal of flexibility and efficiency from the creative team. This affects the role of the choreographer considerably. In this chapter basic guidance is given on how the structure and procedures of this medium work. With experience you will evolve your own approach and priorities.

1. The production company, the client, the agency

2. First contact with the choreographer

3. The contract

4. Preparation

5. The production team

6. Performers, auditions, assistants and rehearsals

7. Shooting/filming

## 1. The production company, the client, the agency

In this context a production company may be one of several 'tendering' or 'pitching' (assembling a package of proposals) for a contract to produce a commercial to advertise a certain product, event or service. The product, represented by 'The Client', could be, for example, a health drink and its manufacturer, or the range of services offered by a bank. Between the production company and the client is 'The Agency' which has written the commercial—the theme, plot or set of visual ideas. The agency selects from competing tenders the production company best suited to work with the client. The production company makes the agency's concepts or plot work successfully and may contribute ideas of its own.

## 2. First contact with the choreographer

The first approach to you may come from a production company which has contacted your agent. The company may know something of your choreographic output or it may be responding to your professional reputation. This could either be at the tendering stage or after the production company has been awarded the contract to make the commercial. If the inclusion of a choreographer is a last minute decision, an offer could come as late as the day before the shoot (the filming day).

The choreographer might be invited to contribute ideas while a proposal is being prepared. If you are called to meetings to discuss ideas, it is unlikely that any speculative work on your part will attract a fee. Ideas which seem to be

taking shape could still change even if 'your' production company wins the contract.

## 3. The contract

If your production company is successful, and if you haven't already contacted your agent, ask if he or she will handle the contract. You will want to know whether the commercial is for television and/or for cinema release, and how that affects your fee. It is likely that an all-inclusive fee for your work will be negotiated with the agency. Overtime is not recognised in this sort of contract (though it would be for any performers involved). The agency will probably negotiate a 'buy-out' arrangement with you whereby it secures all rights to use the commercial for a specified period and in specified countries. Choreographers in this field do not usually receive royalties.

## 4. Preparation

You may have three or four weeks to prepare and rehearse your choreographic ideas or just one day. This depends on when you were contacted and the amount of choreography needed within the commercial.

Establish the length of the commercial and whether it is to be shot in a film studio or on location. Ask the production company to supply you with a storyboard if there is one. A 'storyboard' is a series of pictures with script, resembling a strip-cartoon in its format, which illustrates in frozen moments the basic 'story' of the commercial to be made. The storyboard could also be a video or animated film. Instead of a storyboard there may be a short script. Ask for a copy.

If you have a recognisable rehearsal

period make sure you will be involved in sufficient meetings and that you are clear about your choreographic contribution. Meetings are likely to be attended by many combinations of contributors, some of whom might be:

✦ The producer of the production company

✦ The director of the production company

✦ The director of the commercial (who may be a freelance film director)

✦ Members of the creative team who write the story and work for the agency

✦ The designer

✦ The musical director

✦ The production manager

✦ The lighting cameraman or woman

Try to assess whether you will be required to motivate the performers, give physical form, drama and visual impact to the director's ideas, or whether you will be expected to create a scene or a short plot, or a series of split-second actions to match each frame of the storyboard from which the director will choose material. You may be asked to devise two versions of the same idea and a choice will be made as to which is best. Sometimes this choice is only finalised during the 'rehearsal with camera' on the shoot day.

## 5. The production team

Ask the agency and the production company for a production team personnel list with job definitions attached to enable you to know in advance who you will be working with and who to approach regarding money, casting, rehearsals, shooting schedules, props, catering and transport. Try to understand and respect the production hierarchy. The director will direct the commercial ('make it happen'). In the studio or on location you are answerable to and collaborate with him, although you would normally communicate via the first or second assistant director. Try to learn the relevant jargon and technical vocabulary so that you can converse with understanding. It is worth noting that in this field of work the choreographer is usually classified as part of the production team.

## 6. Performers, auditions, assistants and rehearsals

If trained dancers, or actors who move well, are needed for your choreography, ask about the audition procedure:

✦ Is it part of your job to find performers?

✦ How many can you invite to be contracted?

✦ Is it part of your job to quote the fee offered to the performers?

✦ Will it be your responsibility to organise the date, time, length and location of the audition or casting session?

✦ Who writes and distributes the audition notice and where is it placed?

✦ Who hires a studio in which to hold

auditions?

✦ Who contacts performers' agencies or individual artists?

✦ Have you planned exactly what form the audition or selection procedure will take?

✦ Who will notify performers of the result of the audition, and when?

You may need to work alongside a casting director who is simultaneously casting principal actors. If dancers or actors have already been selected ask for a list of names and addresses and ask to meet them in advance of rehearsals or the shoot. You will want to find out who can move well and you may also want to assess such things as height, physical appearance, physical strength, voice, musicality and personality.

Do you need an assistant for the auditions or, indeed, for the whole engagement? If you do, make this clear to the production company and agency as soon as possible. If the budget precludes the engagement of an assistant find out what sort of practical support is available from members of the production team.

Ask whether you can schedule some rehearsals prior to filming (though this may depend on the size of the production budget) or whether you will be expected to choreograph everything on the day of filming.

## 7. Shooting/filming

Shooting days start early and are very long. If you anticipate a transport problem (you have no car, the journey is difficult, or the proposed hours of work will create a professional problem) it is advisable to discuss transport when your contract is being negotiated. You may not be offered the services of a company driver to take you to a distant location for the shoot, but if you are, consider any advantages carefully before declining in favour of your own transport. You may be offered reimbursement for your petrol or fares.

Take plenty of warm clothes if you know you will be working in unheated surroundings or in the open air. Ask in advance about catering facilities on location, especially if you have particular dietary needs.

If your only rehearsal time takes place on the day of filming, make some enquiries about what sort of facilities will be provided and specify what you need. At the very least, check the provision of a CD player or tape recorder with a counter to facilitate speedy rehearsals. Find out whether you will have to rehearse on the set while it is being built, working in amongst cables and other obstructions. Is there a separate rehearsal room of adequate size and temperature? Are there any dressing-rooms and toilet facilities?

During the shoot, in addition to all other participants, the client and several members of the agency may also be present. They could interfere with the carefully-prepared structure of the commercial and make changes of any sort at the last minute. Some decisions may, therefore, be taken out of the hands of the director and may necessitate changes in the choreography. Be prepared to respond and adapt quickly to changes which come about.

You would not normally be required to attend the editing process for a commercial but you could ask to observe. Ask

for a tape of the commercial to be sent
to you after it has been edited, since it
could be useful in your own promotional
portfolio.

*See also:*
**Contract** (page 3)

**Working abroad:**
Translator (page 107)
Insurance (page 105)

**Working as a choreographer:**
Casting (Availability of performers)
(page 41)
Audition procedure (page 41)
Rehearsals (Facilities) (page 35)
(Personal equipment) (page 37)

**Assistants, notators and staff
producers** (page 111)

**Money** (page 11)

# Working as a choreographer for television: three examples

Rapid and constant technological developments in the medium have meant that opportunities for the recording of choreo-graphy specially for television are increasing. This chapter selects three settings in which a choreographer might work for— or in—television, in circumstances where a source of advice on practice, contracts and fees may be useful.

The chapter does not discuss the nature of collaboration with a television director, a design team and musicians, nor the rights of those collaborators. It does not give an analysis of how a television camera will affect your choreography, or break down the role of various television personnel.

The three settings discussed are:

✦ recording an extract of an existing choreographic work

✦ recording the whole of an existing choreographic work

✦ being commissioned to create choreography specifically for television

The examples range from one where there may be a lack of time for preparation or adjust-ment to the medium (recording an extract of an existing work) to one in which the medium will be at the heart of your work (being specially commissioned).

1. Recording an extract of an existing choreographic work

2. Recording the whole of an existing choreographic work

3. Choreographic com-missions for television

4. General notes

5. Editing

6. Contracts

## 1. Recording an extract of an existing choreographic work

*A television company or broadcaster approaches you with a request to record a short extract (normally five minutes or less) of a named choreographic work. The work may be one you are presently rehearsing that has not yet been seen in public, or an existing work in rehearsal for representation.*

You may be interested to know whether the short extract will be shown as part of a news bulletin, magazine programme, specialist arts series or other type of programme, and when it will be shown. Find out the length of the extract planned.

In the case of an existing work, find out if the director has recorded dance before and if he or she has already seen the full work in performance. It might also be helpful to know to what extent he or she is familiar with your choreographic output, as this will help you to assess your input.

Time for discussion about the recording of a short extract is likely to be limited, so it may help the director if you specify (or suggest) the short section of choreography which may be the most effective and practical to record in the circumstances. It will be a great advantage if you have a sense of what looks good on camera. Bear in mind that on the day of recording it may be necessary for the dancers to repeat the extract many times before the final 'take', so choose a section which will look attractive but not be utterly exhausting.

Find out where and when the recording will take place—your rehearsal or performance venue or the television company's studio—and whether the dancers should wear rehearsal clothes or full costume.

Find out whether there is any provision for a warm-up or run-through within the time allocated for the recording session.

Under the BBC Equity Agreement, the payment for an extract depends on its length. For an extract of under two minutes transmission time to be broadcast on a news or magazine programme there is no payment (in this case, the extract is seen to be valuable promotion of your work that will benefit you or your company). Over two minutes, payment is due at different rates according to transmission length. If you are approached by an independent production company who do not operate under Equity guidelines, or use a different contract, the payment procedure will differ.

If you are also dancing in the work, a performance fee will be payable. This is calculated according to the type of programme. You will also be paid an attendance fee for each recording session, pre- and post-production meeting and editing session at which you are present. This payment might be a negotiable lump sum.

## 2. Recording the whole of an existing choreographic work

*A television production company approaches you with a request to record an existing work.*

The over-all approach of the director or production company should provide some indication of the nature of their proposed investment in your work. Before you sign a contract, arrange sufficient meetings with both the director and production company to ensure that a fruitful working relationship can develop and that you understand each other's working methods. Get the director to explain his or her intentions with regard to the presentation of your work. Ask in what context, or programme 'slot', it will be broadcast.

Together you will look at the 'scratch tape' in order to discuss the shape and structure of the original dance work and the recording. A scratch tape is a high quality video of a recent performance of the choreography in question, shot plainly and under adequate lighting conditions from the back of the stalls (rather than a video made of the work that contains shots from the side of the stage or any effects in addition to the choreography itself). If the dance company does not automatically make a scratch tape, make sure you make one with the cast that will be used for the small screen recording.

There are two ways in which existing choreography is recorded:

✦ Relayed from a public performance

✦ Re-staged specifically for camera

Make sure you discuss which method of recording is applicable to your work at an early stage.

Discussion will take place with regard to rehearsal dates and times, rehearsal locations and the recording schedule. Make sure that if adjustments are to be made to the original choreography for it to suit the medium, sufficient rehearsal time is available to you with the complete cast. Check that on the day of recording there is time and a suitable space for a preliminary warm-up or class.

If not automatically given to you, ask for copies of rehearsal and shooting schedules.

## 3. Choreographic commissions for television

*You are offered the opportunity to create an entirely new work specifically for the small screen in collaboration with a director and design team.*

If you have offered a proposal for a dance work for the camera, the production company or broadcaster will have chosen your ideas because of their feasibility and innovation in the medium. In order to produce such a proposal you will have worked with a director. The nature of this collaboration will depend on both parties' experience: an experienced director and an inexperienced choreographer may make the collaboration unequal (though very instructive). Make sure you work with a director who is prepared to listen to your ideas. It will be helpful if you begin to learn the language of television before you start to collaborate.

In this context, either the commissioning television company will own your work, or it will be owned by the co-producers (for example a national funding body which has funded a specific series of arts programmes and the television company). The choreographer and director may receive an identical fee.

The television company or co-producers may negotiate a licence that allows them the total rights to one or more showings in the UK and abroad over a specific period. The company will want to re-coup its investment through overseas and cable sales. There could be a restrictive clause in your contract that prevents

81

you from making the same work for another television company, or from presenting it 'live' before its television premiere. If you want to use some of the choreographic material from a television commission for further development in a live production, it is wise to discuss this possibility with the television company which owns the rights to the work in its original form.

## 4. General notes

The director-choreographer relationship can be a very creative partnership, at its best founded on good preparation and communication accompanied by a flexible approach to the task.

If you are unfamiliar with video and television, the use of a video camera in other rehearsals, used as a 'video notebook', will help you learn what does and doesn't work on the screen. A choreographer's time-consuming attention to a small physical detail may irritate a director if the adjustment seems relatively unimportant to the overall shot. Time is money, particularly with regard to the use of film and employment of camera crews, but it is important that you have opportunities to express your point of view and any concerns about the way the choreography is being shot.

You will be approached by a television company to make a 'recording' of your choreography rather than a film or a video. It will then be decided which format to use - a decision based on time, budget, aesthetic and practical concerns. Video is the cheaper medium and allows you to see the result of the shot immediately, whereas film has to be sent away to be processed. If shooting on film, ask for video-assisted view-finders to al-

low you to see the output of the camera as it is being rehearsed and shot. Though the choreographic work might be shot on film, post-production is frequently done on video.

When recording is taking place from a theatre, it is normal for the choreographer to watch the recording in a room away from the director, but making notes as the recording progresses for discussion afterwards. If shooting on location or in the rehearsal studio it is normal for the director and choreographer to work together using video-assisted viewing. If the recording is being made in a television studio, the director will be in the gallery, well-away from the studio floor. Discuss with him or her where it is best for you to be. This is often on the studio floor looking at an output monitor with headphones and talk-back facilities so that you can discuss shots immediately with the director. In this case your main point of contact will be the floor manager who is responsible for organisation and safety on the studio floor.

When you are working in the television studio ask for a pair of headphones and a script. This will enable you to hear the shot numbers being called and you can mark on the script any queries or problems you may have while you watch the monitor. This numerical co-ordination will help in discussions with the director.

Make sure you introduce yourself and your dancers to the camera crew as well as the floor manager. Plotting shots in a studio situation is a slow and boring process. Convey to your dancers the importance of stopping and standing in the exact spot when asked to stop.

As choreographer insist on being present at a recording session. If you cannot attend, ensure that you are represented by someone you trust who can approve the way in which your work is being represented.

## 5. Editing

You will not have ultimate editorial control over the final visual presentation of the choreography, but may be invited to contribute to the editorial process. The degree to which your opinion or presence is required at the editorial stage should be specified in your contract.

The choreographer is not seen as a hindrance in the cutting room in most cases, though this may depend on the personal relationship established throughout the recording process. Some directors may find your presence helpful at this stage. Take the chance to be involved in cutting and editing decisions, since the opportunity may be very instructive and could help you gain more control over the final appearance of the choreography. It will also complete your experience of the whole television recording process.

## 6. Contracts

If you do not have the services of an agent or manger when approached by a television production company, seek qualified professional advice when checking your contract. You could also discuss matters with a colleague who is experienced in the medium.

A television company will want to buy the licence to record and broadcast your choreography. They will either negotiate a fee based upon the number of minutes of screen time payable each time the choreography is shown, or (more likely)

offer an over-all fee—a 'buy-out'—for a specific or indefinite number of showings over a specific period as described in the contract.

✦ Check that the description of the commission in your contract is what you expected as a result of preparatory discussion and negotiation.

✦ Check the rehearsal schedule and locations, and the recording schedule and locations.

✦ Are you expected, or do you want, to be present at the recording?

✦ Are you required, or do you want, to attend the editing session(s)?

✦ Check the payment date and arrangements for your fee.

✦ Check the payment of any necessary travel and/or accommodation expenses. This is especially important if you live and work (or are on tour) in the north of Britain, for example, and the television studios are in the south. When are these expenses payable?

International rights for overseas broadcasting will most likely be negotiated (and paid for) at a later stage by the production company. Alternatively, these may be negotiated, or exploitation of these rights made, during the pre-production stage and the responsibility for paying any third party rights agreed between the production company and its partner or purchaser.

After the expiry of the initial term of

exploitation, the rights may be re-negotiated if the television company sees a new
market for the product.

*See also:*
**Contract** (page 3)

**Working as a choreographer for an
advertising commercial** (page 74)

**Videotapes** (page 139)

**Copyright** (page 151)

**Useful addresses:**
The Place - Video Place (booklet)

# Working as a choreographer with schools and youth organisations

This chapter has a wide application. It considers a choreographer's involvement in:

✦ a professional production using children with formal dance training

✦ a professional production using children without formal dance training

✦ an amateur production with people of all ages (although the advice in this chapter is more applicable to projects or productions for people over seven years) who may or may not have dance training or experience

✦ various branches of 'educational' work

The range of advice offered here reflects the breadth of current theatrical and educational work, as well as the imaginative and varied approach of individual choreographers and advisers.

1.  What sort of choreographic work is expected?

2.  Your contract or formal agreement

3.  Future use of the choreography

4.  Co-operation of parents, school or community staff

5.  Double casting and understudies

6.  Attendance at rehearsals or workshops

7.  People with special needs

8.  Facilities, supervision and assistance

9.  Costume

10. Final or stage rehearsal

11. Pre-performance warm-up or rehearsal

## 1. What sort of choreographic work is expected?

A youth or community group, school, college, or regional dance festival may want a professional choreographer to work with children, young people or people involved in some form of collective education on a dance project. The organisers' expectations need to be identified and made known to, or discussed with, the choreographer:

+ What is the proposed work going to be?

+ What are the participants' expectations?

+ How many participants will be involved?

+ Are they of a mixed age range?

+ Are they of mixed abilities?

+ How much dance experience, if any, do they have?

+ Is a professional choreographer's approach appropriate for the job?

+ How much should the participants be encouraged to contribute to the choreographic process?

+ Is the organiser expecting a professional work with very high aesthetic and physical standards?

+ How broadly should the project appeal to the range of participants, and in what cultural, social, musical and/or physical respects?

+ Should the work be choreographed 'on' the group?

+ Is a public performance expected, or desirable? If so, how many performances?

> *Sometimes it is important and rewarding to assess 'achievement' by looking at where and what you started with, rather than looking for a complete and polished project or production.*
>
> Denni Sayers, choreographer

In preliminary discussions, establish exactly why the project is taking place: Are the young people involved in order to gain a creative educational experience, to learn a particular technique or to answer a curricular demand for the arts? Is the experience intended to be therapeutic? Don't feel pressed towards a public performance if performing, particularly in public, is not an important part of the work. A video recording might reflect the children's 'achievement' and be more appropriate and useful for teachers, parents and other organisers. If the project has been commercially sponsored or funded by, for example, a regional arts board, check in the conditions of that funding whether a public performance is expected, and ask if a video recording of the work would be acceptable instead.

What form should the project take? Should it be a residency, series of workshops, period of technique classes or a mixture of all of these? What kind of follow-up activities are expected, and over what period of time?

Insufficient discussion and understanding can result in a situation where the choreographer's arrival to lead a workshop at a school seems to indicate a 'morning off'. Potentially helpful teachers are not present to supervise the children or support the choreographer's work. Attendance numbers are low.

*See also:*
**Working as a choreographer in the community** (page 92)

**Useful addresses:** National Dance Agencies (Yorkshire Dance Centre) (booklet)

## 2. Your contract or formal agreement

It is advisable to check through the chapters <u>Working as a choreographer</u>, <u>Money</u> and <u>Contract</u> in conjunction with the points mentioned in this section:

✦ Is the proposed fee appropriate, and is it for the creation of the choreography including any preparation or research?

✦ Is there a production budget which is quite separate from your fee? Do you have control of this budget?

✦ Have you got enough time to involve all participants in the creative process?

✦ Are you expected to select or audition participants, or will you involve anyone who turns up on the first day?

✦ Do you need a professional or other assistant? If so, can this be afforded by the production budget?

✦ Are you and the participants covered by the school's insurance—in school hours and after? Make enquiries and check your own personal and public liability insurance.

*See also:* **Insurance** (page 145)

Although you may, as a professional choreographer, be obliged to make some concessions with regard to your normal contractual arrangements, it is still advisable to secure agreements in writing.

Some educational organisers have commented that choreographers charge too high a fee for community and education groups to afford. It might seem that a fully professional job is expected for a lesser fee. Make sure that the organisers or educational institution understand that your commitment, though willing, cannot necessarily be one which supports the work in a charitable way.

## 3. Future use of the choreography

Make sure that you own the choreographic copyright. Secure in your contract provision for consultation in the event of further use or performance or adaptation of your work. You may be available to revive or adapt your work but you will want to know if a fee will be forthcoming for the work involved. You may feel content to leave any necessary adaptations to a nominated assistant or teacher.

You may decide to develop a choreographic work created for those in vocational training, or for a community youth group, into a larger work for a professional company. The expansion of the work may not have been foreseen at the start, but if you pursue the idea, the original group will lose what it may have prized as an important element of exclusivity. If your proposed development of their work does proceed legitimately, it would be considerate (and perhaps of historic interest) if you were to include acknowledgement to the original performing group, venue and date, in subsequent publicity and programme material for the new work. You should first check the terms of your original agreement with the group or school.

## 4. Co-operation of parents, school or community staff

You may be contracted to join a project's creative production team after the consent and co-operation of staff and parents to the children's participation has been obtained (at least in principle). Build on this foundation by meeting the staff most closely involved, and by being prepared to discuss the project and your ideas and to offer any reassurances which may be necessary.

You will need the consent of parents and teachers if school time will be missed through attendance at your rehearsals. Co-operation may well be needed for attendance at evening and weekend rehearsals, performances and costume fittings.

Many choreographers have pointed out the necessity to respect school timetable demands and work within these restrictions. In order to change times, places and dates of rehearsals, the school will usually communicate with parents or guardians by letter with a return slip seeking their permission for any new or extra-curricular activities. The process of sending and collecting returned letters may take two to three weeks.

*See also:*
**Child performance regulations**
(page 162)

Socialising with a large number of parents can be demanding, and though desirable, is not always practical or possible. One way to meet parents briefly is to be visible and available to talk when they collect their children from the school, community centre, theatre or rehearsal space. Consider the feasibility of some 'open' rehearsals if you are asked to allow parents to attend.

It might be helpful if, in collaboration with a parent or teacher, you prepared an information sheet for parents or guardians listing some basic details. The school might agree to reproduce and distribute this information:

✦ What is involved?

✦ When are the workshops or rehearsals?

✦ Where are rehearsals and/or performances to take place?

✦ How long do sessions last?

✦ Should the children bring food?

✦ Is any particular clothing necessary?

You may want to collaborate with teachers or adult participants in some way with regard to the theme of your project or production. There may be participants with a keen interest in, for instance, dance, drama, sport, social or cultural studies, history or geography, language or literature. These people could become researchers and collaborators for the project.

## 5. Double casting and understudies

Find out at the earliest opportunity whether the production must have two (or more) complete casts or double casting for certain roles. Discover whether double casting is a legal requirement (as may be the case in professional theatre) or for the benefit and experience of the children. Assess whether it is practical or possible to teach two casts at once, or separately, or whether your assistant (if you have one) could help with this. Remember that the children in an alternative cast who are not necessarily trained or inclined to watch and learn from others will need separate time and attention to learn their parts. Be aware that if children remember very little choreography or music from one rehearsal to another, a proportion of each rehearsal will be used to remember what was created the previous day. Your choreographic progress may be slower than you originally planned.

Make sure that it is absolutely clear whether a child is an alternative cast and will perform at specified performances, or whether the child is the understudy of a specified role ready to replace that child in the event of sickness or accident. Make sure that the production team (particularly the costume department), parents, teachers and other collaborators are also quite clear about these arrangements.

## 6. Attendance at rehearsals or workshops

It is worth being reminded that not all the children or young people involved in a large-scale community project or production will be able or inclined to attend your rehearsals with regularity, especially during school holidays. You will rarely have your complete cast available when you most want it because there will be children absent for dental appointments, religious observance, sports events, weddings, holidays, lack of transport and responsibilities at home as well as forgetfulness. Try to secure their special co-operation and commitment to stage rehearsals and final rehearsals and explain the mutual benefits.

It could be helpful to instigate a rehearsal register so that you and others

can see who is present and who is not, although it may not be appropriate to take such a public role-call if attendance is voluntary. If it is appropriate, however, an attendance register can also help you learn people's names quickly. Make sure everyone knows where the register or signing-in sheet is located and explain why it should be used. This register could also be of importance in the event of an emergency evacuation.

## 7. People with special needs

Before starting work ask the school or staff if any of the young people have disabilities, especially conditions which may not be immediately apparent to you, the newcomer. Try to get helpful background information on the needs of those with, for example, diabetes, epilepsy, partial or no hearing, poor sight, recently damaged limbs, wheelchair users. Consider whether you need to undertake some further research or preliminary workshops. Would the services of a sign-language interpreter, or a teacher or parent with this skill, be helpful for your work? What are the participants' capabilities and aspirations?

## 8. Facilities, supervision and assistance

If you plan to spend several weeks or months working with, for instance, 100 children, do not agree to rehearse in any recommended hall or warehouse without visiting it first, unless you have received detailed assurances concerning its facilities from someone who has fully inspected the space and whose judgement you trust. Pay particular attention to the floor surface, temperature, ventilation, light, electricity supply, safety and security matters, emergency exits, changing-rooms and toilets, drinking water, car parking and access and waiting area for parents.

Remember that 100 children cannot use one toilet or drinking-fountain in a ten-minute break. 100 children cannot be expected to return to rehearsal in ten minutes if the one sweet shop in the area is reached by a fifteen minute stroll.

Discuss the provision of refreshment during rehearsals. Can the children bring packed lunches or will the catering be organised by the school, venue or theatre? Can the children eat their packed lunches somewhere other than on the rehearsal floor?

100 children will generate a lot of noise and will need to be supervised arriving and departing, resting and eating. Your voice may not be heard by everyone in a large group in a vast unfurnished warehouse or in a field. You may need amplification equipment. It is not uncommon to find that large industrial fan-heaters are provided to heat halls or warehouses where re-hearsals take place. Choreographers and directors have found their voices cannot be heard above the roar of the blowers, and when the fan-heaters are turned off the space very quickly becomes cold. You may want to divide the cast into smaller and more manageable groups in order to teach efficiently.

*See also:* **Working as a choreographer:** Rehearsals (Facilities) (page 35)

## 9. Costume

Whether or not you are working with a designer, this element of the production may require your additional respon-sibility. You will want to schedule adequate time for fittings during the rehearsal period. You will also need to explain to everyone concerned the need for the children to arrive at the per-formance venue with sufficient time to prepare hair-styles, head-dresses, face or body make-up and to dress in costume. Extra helpers may be needed. Try to provide your helpers with information in advance about costume, hair and make-up in order to help their understanding and speed (very often in a confined space). Find out where the changing-rooms are and check the facilities.

## 10. Final or stage rehearsals

Whether your production takes place indoors or outside, remember that if your choreography will eventually be inte-grated with staging for other performers you must try to secure sufficient rehearsal time for the transition from rehearsal space to performing area, for rehearsing children alone, and for the integration of the children with other professional or amateur performers such as singers, actors, dancers and acrobats for example. This is rarely a straightforward procedure and, although pressed for time, you may want or be asked to adjust your choreography. There may be problems of access to the stage or entrances. There may be staging and technical difficulties. There may be no concealed space for quick-changes of costume. The co-operation and interest of the children is more likely to be retained if you have explained in advance the probable need for changes during the final stages of production preparation.

In fully professional productions, children and young people are often required to attend a series of stage or final rehearsals of, typically, three hours duration, though their attendance time might be shorter according to regulations. Their participation is needed but at an unspecified moment and when that moment comes it only lasts a few minutes. In these cases, the children will need to wait somewhere. Rehearsal delays are often unavoidable, so check what facilities are available and arrange supervision. It may be possible to rehearse while waiting around, in which case you may delegate this to an assistant (if you are needed elsewhere). You may need a piano, pianist, member of chorus staff, other musicians and musical instruments, tape recorder and rehearsal props to make the rehearsal productive.

## 11. Pre-performance warm-up or rehearsal

The need for any pre-performance warm-up or rehearsal may be difficult to predict during the planning stages of a production and will depend on the nature of the production and participants. However, it is worth warning all relevant production and administration staff that this may be necessary. Make it clear that you would like to assess the need during the rehearsal period and then discuss how a warm-up could be achieved.

Points to think about:

✦ How efficient is the collective physical, musical and dramatic memory of the group?

✦ Would it be useful or necessary to run-through sections of music, singing, dancing and stylised movement before each performance?

✦ If this is necessary, which members of staff, teachers or parents will conduct or supervise these preparation

sessions? Is it the choreographer's responsibility?

✦ Where and when can such rehearsals and 'notes' sessions take place?

✦ If no rehearsal is necessary, is a quiet place and time needed for the children to settle after their school activities and focus on the production?

*See also:*
**Contract** (page 3)

**Working as a choreographer:**
Casting (page 39)
Audition procedure (page 41)

**Money** (page 11)

**Child performance regulations** (page 162)

**Assistants, notators and staff producers** (page 111)

**Music** (page 120)

**Health and safety** (page 156)

**Working as a choreographer in the community** (page 92)

**Insurance** (page 145)

**Set and costume design** (page 130)

**Useful publications:**
Regular Marvels (booklet)

# Working as a choreographer in the community

A choreographer working in the field of community dance needs to be able to share a process with people who might not have the same understanding of the dance world, 'choreography' or other terms that are applied in the rest of this guide. At the heart of this work is the requirement to meet the needs of the people you are working with, and to choreograph using content that arises from the process of working with a particular group. This work may require a different set of skills from those employed by choreographers working in the commercial theatre. It is important, however, to read Working as a choreographer, Money and Contract, since the information given in these chapters is likely to form the basis of your negotiations.

This section has been written by Linda Jasper, Chair of the Community Dance & Mime Foundation, Lecturer in Dance and Professional Training Tutor in the Department of Dance Studies at the University of Surrey, on behalf of CDMF.

1. Who do you work with?

2. How is the work done?

3. Is a performance appropriate?

4. Fees, contracts and cancellations

5. Insurance

6. Production costs

7. How to get experience

Many choreographers in the community dance profession practise in a variety of dance genres. Some have full-time posts as community dance workers, dancers-in-residence or dance artists/teachers in community companies. Others are freelance and work on a project basis. In addition, some of the education units attached to the larger dance companies employ choreographers to devise particular projects.

## 1. Who do you work with?

This varies greatly depending on the sort of community group you may be working with. It can be, for example, a group of twenty young dancers who meet weekly in a youth centre, an integrated dance group of able and disabled dancers, a group of old people who meet in a day centre, or a mixed age, gender and ability group of people who are brought together for an intensive project during a holiday period. The time scale of the creative period varies. The ages, gender, dance abilities and requirements are different depending on the project. If used to working with dancers who have a common training it may be an adjustment for some choreographers to work with 'untrained' dancers who fall outside what is conventionally considered to be a 'dancer' (female, under thirty, very physically able and expected to convey the choreographer's requirements through a rehearsal period into a public performance). Dancers who work on community projects often have bodies which are perhaps young and lacking in physical training, or old, and may have a disability.

Responding to bodies that have not necessarily been trained into familiar movement patterns does have many advantages in extending the movement range of the choreographer, allowing them to perceive movement differently. For some choreographers this might be a difficult adjustment to make.

## 2. How is the work done?

Apart from an intensive project, which might occur over a holiday period, many groups meet weekly in their leisure time, so that intervals between sessions might be quite extended. This leads to work which might be developed more slowly. The nature of the choreography might be affected by other events which occur to the participants between sessions. In addition, it is not possible to guarantee that everyone will be able to prioritise the session over other important demands in their lives. This requires the choreographer to be particularly flexible and responsive to the changing dynamics within the group.

Choreographers who work through improvisation, use pedestrian movements, set tasks or games to derive movement ideas, may have more skills to bring to this area than choreographers who prefer to work out sections of choreography in the studio with relatively little opportunity for the dancers to alter the choreography or contribute to its creation.

The choreographer's role is one that is negotiated between the group involved, the facilitator/project co-ordinator and community dance worker. Some groups who are experienced in their own choreographic work might want an 'outside eye' to give advice as to how their work is perceived and how it could be made more effective. Some groups might be just starting and need assistance in helping to find methods of devising movement and shaping it. Other groups might need the experience of working with a choreographer who extends their normal dance range. In the end, it is the group's development that is taken into account when negotiating the nature of the choreographer's role.

## 3. Is a performance appropriate?

For many people a performance might be the highlight, the culmination and sharing of an enjoyable project. However, it is not always appropriate for a choreographic project to end in a performance. A group might feel that it is not something it wants to do, or feel that it is not a natural way of ending the process. There are many reasons for putting on a performance within community dance; it makes visible what is usually a closed project to a wider world. Funding bodies might require an opportunity for the public recognition of their support, and, indeed, the community dance worker and/or the choreographer might need to show their choreography in public to provide evidence of the quality of the work in order to raise support for future projects.

*See also:*

**Working as a choreographer in schools and youth organisations** (page 85)

## 4. Fees, contracts and cancellations

If you are working on a freelance basis for a community dance project, fees are negotiable and variable depending on the nature of the work and the organisation for whom you are working.

There are no specific guidelines for fees other than those suggested by Equity. If in doubt, ask other choreographers working in the field and regional arts board officers about the usual rates of payment. It is always sensible to state clearly the fee to be paid in a contract or letter of agreement. Sometimes projects have to be cancelled at short notice due to a lack of public response, or lack of funding. Make sure that your contract provides for compensation should cancellation occur.

Try to assess the amount of time and expense involved in travelling to and from venue, hall or studio when the project involves sessions that are unpredictable in terms of their length and frequency.

Many aspects of work within the community dance sector are outlined in CDMF's *Regular Marvels*, a handbook for animateurs, practitioners and development workers in dance, mime, music and literature.

*See also:*
**Money** (page 11)

**Contract** (page 3)

Useful publications:
Regular Marvels (booklet)

## 5. Insurance

You will need personal and equipment insurance (for musical instruments, clothing and sound equipment) when working in community dance. Ensure that the venue/organisation has public liability and equipment insurance to cover the group's activities. The hiring organisation or venue should have its own insurance to cover your work, but check, and if it does not then take out a policy through a broker. Do not assume that insurance has been secured.

*See also:* **Insurance** (page 145)

## 6. Production costs

Money for production costs is often limited. It is challenging to raise money for projects in community dance, which are often financed through partnership funding from a number of sources (local authorities, regional arts boards, business sponsorship and individual participant contributions). Securing money for costumes, scenery, props and special effects is unlikely. Most community dance performances are costumed and produced very economically. It is advisable to ask about any limitations in the production budget at the beginning of the project.

## 7. How to get experience

Choreographers wishing to find out where community dance opportunities might lie should contact their local dance development officer, dance animateur or dancer-in-residence. Names of most practitioners in the UK can be found in the Community Dance & Mime Foundation's *Network* brochure. Go and see work being done with local youth groups in schools and in day centres. Watch performances of work, to assess how far you are interested in working in this way and what you might be able to contribute to the field. Regional arts boards have policies which allocate funds for artists to work with amateur and community groups. Find out if they have funded a project that you could observe.

The most effective way of getting experience in this area is to observe and work alongside experienced choreographers with a good track record in community work. Regional Arts Boards and the English, Welsh, Scottish and Northern Irish Arts Councils might offer training bursaries to cover 'mentoring' schemes (on which the trainee works under the eye of a more established choreographer) or placements attached to a community dance project, independent choreographer, national dance agency or company working in the community. Short courses are available on group work skills and working with the community. Such training may enhance the skills of choreographers hoping to work in this way. CDMF has information on training courses nationally and can offer guidelines on setting up placements and mentor schemes.

*See also:*
**Useful addresses:**
CDMF (booklet)
National Dance Agencies (Yorkshire Dance Centre) (booklet)

# Working as a choreographer for a specific site or occasion: organisation

If you are creating a dance work for a special occasion in a venue or environment that is not a conventional theatre or designated performing space, either indoors or outside, you will be aware that the smooth-running of any production—whether in a tent, an empty warehouse or on a seaside pier—depends as much on the technical and administrative organisation of the event as it does on the choreography.

This chapter stresses the preparatory organisation you, or your producer, will have to do in planning an event. The advice contained here supposes that, as a choreographer involved in an unusual event, you may be more concerned with technical and administrative decisions. No assumption is made about the scale or nature of the event and the advice should not be read in isolation from other relevant chapters in the guide.

1. Personnel

2. Insurance

3. Licensing

4. Administrator

5. Budget

6. Technical or production manager

7. Rehearsal and performance site

8. Sound engineer

9. Lighting requirements

10. Audience

11. Publicity

12. First aid

13. Emergency services

14. Get-in and get-out

## 1. Personnel

Consider surrounding yourself with a team with whom you can share responsibilities. If you are working for an organisation (for example, a producer, a supporting management established for the occasion, a local authority or a rural trust) establish the roles which you want to adopt, or will be expected to adopt, as soon as possible. If an administrator and a production manager are already employed for the project, involve them in these discussions.

If you are able to select the people with whom you will work, try to choose people with previous technical and administrative experience in the organisation of a similar event. You may have to consider aspects of licensing and insurance not previously encountered by, for example, an administrator who has only worked in a conventional theatre. You may need to confront the technical and practical aspects of working in an unequipped space which requires detailed preliminary assessment, plans and specifications. In choosing your cast and collaborators, find people who are prepared to give you support while working in unusual and possibly testing circumstances.

## 2. Insurance

You or your administrator should check on all the insurances which may be needed for the venue or environment at which you intend to perform. If necessary, consult a specialist insurance company, preferably one that understands your requirements. Local authorities and their health and safety officers are often able to advise.

When setting up insurance be explicit about everything you intend to do. A larger premium paid is less expensive in the long run than a claim for compensation for something for which you are either not covered or inadequately covered.

You must have:

✦ Employer's Liability

✦ Public Liability

✦ Personal Accident

✦ Equipment insurance (with everything costed at <u>replacement as new</u> value)

You may also need:

✦ Personal Professional

✦ Group Comprehensive

✦ All Risks

✦ Cancellation/Abandonment

✦ Specific insurance for special effects and equipment

*See also:* **Insurance** (page 145)

## 3. Licensing

Your public entertainment licence may not be granted unless health and safety requirements are satisfied.

Try to arrange well in advance meetings with the site owner and/or the local authority, starting with environmental health, health and safety, licensing, and fire officers. These people will usually be helpful in providing guidelines on the conditions your production will need to meet in order to be able to go ahead in public. In return, you should be prepared to supply them with an outline of the type of event planned, and anticipated numbers of people attending. If you have any specific problems, ask these officers for advice on how you can comply with regulations. For example, you will need to satisfy environmental health that noise levels do not exceed the statutory limit. Be aware that each local authority may interpret legislation differently.

You need to consider health and safety matters in terms of rehearsal facilities, the performing area, the performers, staff, and audience as well as the venue. Bear in mind that you might be working in adverse weather conditions.

You need to be able to show the local authority or other organiser that you have undertaken a risk assessment. This means that you have considered and written down in your performance proposal risks and how to solve them — risks in relation to, for example, the rehearsal area, staff, performance area and public.

The local authority and possibly the on-site health and safety officer will be able to advise about fire exits, fire appliances, anchoring of technical equipment and secondary lighting.

*See also:* **Health and safety** (page 156)

## 4. Administrator

If you have no administrative help and have been approached to stage a work for a specific site or occasion be sure to stipulate all your needs. Provide the company or commissioning organisation with your required technical specifications and the working conditions in which you require to rehearse and perform as well as those you will need to have backstage in terms of changing rooms, washing facilities, catering and the provision of transport to and from the site. Try to secure confirmation of all matters in writing.

If you have the services of an administrator, could this person be helped by — and liaise with — people from within the commissioning organisation?

The administration may involve the negotiation of two contracts: one with the promoter securing your services, and one with the venue permitting its use.

You will need a Public Entertainment Licence issued by the local authority. There will be a fee for this which will depend on the size of your venture.

You or the administrator will need to secure contracts for dancers and other performers, for yourself and for the event. Pay particular attention to your choreographic rights and to cancellation clauses in the contract. There may also need to be contracts with the various sub-contractors who provide staging, seating, heating, catering and so on.

Check any contract to see if you are obliged to perform elsewhere in the event of an open air performance being cancelled due to rain or adverse weather conditions. Agree only if you know this will be possible in an alternative venue.

You or the administrator should check on the necessity for a Performing Right Society licence. The venue or site may already have a licence or **may** need one for the particular kind of event you are planning. The PRS will advise.

*See also:*

**Contract** (page 3)

**Money** (page 11)

**Music** (page 120)

## 5. Budget

Almost all matters addressed in this chapter will have some sort of budgetary implication. If it is your responsibility, try to draw up your budget plan as early as possible. The scope of this will affect what is or is not possible artistically. The practical aspects of work on a large scale or in an unusual environment often prove to be more complicated and expensive than expected during initial discussions.

It is an advantage when presenting a budget plan to potential sponsors or sources of funding to show that you have considered all the additional costs that your project may attract. Include a large contingency sum.

## 6. Technical or production manager

A technical or production manager will assess the site or venue and tell you what is feasible in order to meet your artistic needs, and advise you on the necessity for further specialists in rigging, lighting, sound design or staging. Help could be offered with rehearsal and technical schedules. With a broad range of responsibilities throughout the project, a technical or production manager's collaboration often contributes significantly to the success of the venture.

## 7. Rehearsal and performance site

*'I've always felt that every dancer should be able to lay a dance floor. I know that in many small touring groups those people do help to carry and lay flooring and they shouldn't necessarily have to do this. I'm just so aware how crucial it is for a dancer to have a secure surface.'*

Simon Byford, production manager

If different spaces are being used for rehearsals and performance, it may be important that the rehearsal space floor area is identical to the performance floor area. Check on a site visit. If the spaces differ, use floor marking during rehearsal and allow enough time during the first rehearsal in the performance area to make any necessary adjustments (choreographic and technical).

Schedule sufficient time and staff for rigging, construction, rehearsals with furniture, machinery and props. You may need to do this firstly with technical staff and then with technical staff and performers.

✦ Will there need to be any additional heating or cooling brought into the rehearsal building or performance area for the performers, staff and/or audience? How will weather conditions affect the performance?

✦ Do you require dressing rooms, tent facilities or portakabins for changing clothes and/or costumes? Provide details of what you require and the numbers of cast, staff, musicians for which the space is needed.

✦ Is there an adequate supply of hot and cold water, drinking water, washing or showering facilities for all concerned? Will catering facilities be necessary for the rehearsal period? If so, what sort and for how many people? Are there suitable catering facilities nearby?

✦ Is there an adequate power supply for all your needs?

✦ Is there a suitable place for musicians and their instruments to be situated in performance? Is this location equipped with any seating, lighting, power and heating requirements? Is it draught-free and, if necessary, covered?

✦ If your performance site is part of a building in use during the working day, will you require the use of certain other rooms (as changing rooms for example) at night? If these rooms are occupied by local staff during the working day, when could you gain access and under what conditions of use?

Be aware that seating may need to be installed for each performance (and moved between performances) and must comply with local safety regulations.

Discuss with the technical manager the best way to provide a suitable floor surface or to remedy defects in an existing one. The floor will almost certainly affect the choice of footwear for the performers. If using a dance floor, check that it can be exposed to weather and heating conditions.

*See also:*
**Working as a choreographer:**
Rehearsals (Facilities—checklist)
(page 35)

**Set and costume design:**
Items for rehearsal—checklist (page 133)

## 8. Sound engineer

Your technical manager may put you in touch with a sound engineer if this is necessary for the production. If sound plays an important part in your work you will need help to make it heard with good quality and appropriate volume, especially in unusual places. The sound engineer will know how best to cope with freak acoustics and echoes.

The sound engineer can decide what sort of system will be most suitable and will also be able to work within any

guidelines set out by the licensing authority, including any requirements for a public address system.

The sound engineer can attend to communications for rehearsals and performance which might entail the use of radio, a microphone and/or mic/headsets for communication between the choreographer, performers, technical and production staff. He or she can provide the amplification of musicians and/or singers and enable them and the dancers to hear what they need to hear.

## 9. Lighting requirements

In order to comply with regulations, your lighting designer and/or technician will need to consider the following points in addition to his or her artistic requirements:

✦ Secondary or emergency lighting in the event of a power failure

✦ Site lights to assist the public to and from the performance areas

✦ Working lights for non-performance times

✦ Adequate lighting for the cast to move to and from the performance space

✦ Provision of generators or adequate power supply

✦ Assurance that all outdoor equipment is waterproof and properly earthed in accordance with the necessary regulations

For open air productions, lighting and plotting sessions should be scheduled at the same time of day or night as the proposed performance if at all possible, since natural lighting conditions will affect any result.

*See also:* **Lighting design** (page 136)

## 10. Audience

✦ Is there adequate public transport to and from the performance space and clear sign posting day and night?

✦ If the performance is in an inaccessible place, can transport be provided for the audience? Who will organise and advertise this service?

✦ Is there adequate access to the performance site for the anticipated number of motor vehicles, pedestrians, elderly or disabled people?

✦ Are there adequate toilet facilities?

✦ Are there any refreshment facilities for the audience?

✦ Consider the minimum distance required between performance and catering if quiet is needed at any moment in the performance.

✦ Will there be any crèche or child care provision? Is this available to staff and performers as well as audience?

✦ Will the seating allow access for the elderly and people who use wheelchairs?

## 11. Publicity

✦ Will you devise and print your own programmes, posters and publicity leaflets or will the organisers?

✦ Who will supply programme sellers and ushers if this is necessary?

✦ Will the advance publicity be sufficiently comprehensive and incorporate all practical advice for the public? Will it, for example, indicate that the event is a 'promenade' performance or that the seating is on grass or deckchairs?

✦ Does the audience need to be advised to bring cushions, rugs, umbrellas, warm clothes, food?

*See also:*
**Working as a choreographer:**
Publicity (page 46)
Programme credits (page 46)

## 12. First aid

Will you require the presence of the St John Ambulance or Red Cross at the site? If so, make sure you tell your cast where to find these voluntary services in case of need.

## 13. Emergency services

Contact these organisations well in advance of the event. Police and motoring organisations (AA, RAC) will advise about large numbers of spectators and their movement to and from the event, as well as any warning or direction signs needed.

✦ Who will provide car parking space and organise parking and attendants?

✦ Will you require the presence of the fire service?

Please note that an increasing number of police authorities may charge fees (per person and per hour) for, say, traffic duty at a private event. Be prepared to include provision for this in your budget if it is a necessary cost. The police do not charge for advisory meetings if you wish to consult them in advance of your event. The fire services do not charge (1995) to attend an event on stand-by, but may be encouraged to do so in the future.

## 14. Get-in and get-out

✦ What is the access to the site for large vans, lorries and articulated trucks? Is the building in a narrow one-way street? Is the access via tarmac road or over grass? Could vehicles get stuck?

✦ After unloading, where is the nearest available parking for the vehicles if they are to remain with you on or near the site for the duration of the project?

✦ Check the dimensions of all access doors and, if available, lifts for moving the equipment and the set in and out of the building or site.

✦ Are there local staff available and are they qualified to help with loading and unloading?

✦ Do you need any lifting or special carrying equipment (cranes or forklift trucks for example)?

*See also:*

**Working as a choreographer with schools and youth organisations** (page 85)

**Working as a choreographer in the community** (page 92)

**Set and costume design** (page 130)

**Lighting design** (page 136)

# Working abroad

While reading other sections of this guide, you will have come across many matters that must be addressed if you are going to work abroad. This chapter highlights issues that are particularly important when considering the organisation of a period of work in a foreign country, and should be read in conjunction with the rest of the guide.

1. Checking your contract

2. Rehearsals and performers

3. Advice from Equity

4. Insurance

5. Passport

6. Visas and work permits

7. Health advice

8. Translator

9. Public holidays and industrial disputes

10. Consular advice

11. Before you go

If planning to work abroad, contact Equity for advice about any necessity to join a local union before signing any contracts. It may be a condition of your contract that you join the local union for the duration of your contract if the engagement is for more than a prescribed number of weeks.

Before you accept work in a foreign country you will need current information about:

✦ European and international law

✦ Taxation

✦ Currency exchange rates

✦ 'Local' employment regulations or traditions

Consult Equity, a lawyer or other professional advisers with specialist knowledge in these areas.

## 1. Checking your contract

Try to have your contract checked by Equity or another professional organisation before you go abroad. Does the contract specify the legal system to which it refers? Check through your contract thoroughly, including the small print, before you sign. Check:

✦ the fee

✦ the terms of payment

✦ any tax and social security payments to be deducted

✦ the currency in which you will be paid

✦ the performing rights

✦ all dates

✦ the subsistence allowance

✦ the travel allowance

✦ the travel and accommodation arrangements

✦ any music matters

✦ the royalty and residual arrangements

✦ local or national taxes

✦ whether you need to join a union

✦ the choreographic copyright

Try to ensure that your contract includes the recording of your work either in movement notation or on video.

If you are already working abroad and you are offered a contract for more work, or work with another company, contact your agent to check the document before you accept the offer. If you are keen to accept work or are under pressure to do so, accept 'subject to contract' whilst your agent scrutinises the offer.

Look for any tax deductions which may be mentioned in the contract, and take qualified advice about any reciprocal tax agreements which may apply to citizens of the UK.

*See also:*
**Money:**
Choreographic fee—deductions
(page 13)

If you are working abroad and experience administrative delay in the delivery of agreed payments, take a colleague with you on your next visit to the finance department (a colleague who has been paid). The company's embarrassment may solve the problem before you consider any further action. If the difficulty tends to arise at the company's bank, take a member of the company's finance or contract staff with you.

*See also:*
**Contract** (page 3)

**Money:**
Choreographic fee —payment
(page 12)
Royalties and residuals (page 12)
Expenses (Travel) (page 14)

**Working as a choreographer:**
Travel arrangements (page 42)
Accommodation arrangements
(page 43)

## 2. Rehearsals and performers

If you haven't already been provided with the information, make enquiries about rehearsal facilities. Check that you understand any rehearsal schedules sent to you in advance. Double check the availability of performers.

If children are involved in your production, make contact with the school or the theatre's children's manager and find out about the regulations which will apply to the inclusion and availability of children or young people in that country.

*See also:*
**Working as a choreographer:**
Rehearsals (Schedules) (page 34)
(Facilities—checklist) (page 35)
Casting (Availability of performers)
(page 41)

**Child performance regulations**
(page 162)

**Assistants, notators and staff producers** (page 111)

## 3. Advice from Equity

United Kingdom-based choreographers should see the <u>overseas addendum</u> which has been agreed by Equity and the theatre management bodies. In addition to covering travel, subsistence and insurance, there is a section on television and film recording when abroad—often a tricky subject. The addendum also covers work in the Republic of Ireland. You are recommended to read the chapter 'Working Abroad' in Equity's *Advice and Rights Guide.*

*See also:*
**Useful publications** (booklet)

**Equity:**
Equity services (page 26)

It may be useful to contact the local centre of the International Theatre Institute in the countries which you will visit. Equity strongly advises its members to make preliminary contact with local unions when planning to work abroad before entering contractual arrangements. Practical assistance can also be sought from the many unions in countries affiliated to the International Federation of Actors. Contact the Equity office for details.

*See also:*
**Money:**
Union membership (page 17)

**Useful addresses** (booklet)

## 4. Insurance

In addition to making sure that you are fully covered by the host company or venue's insurance, check that you have the necessary professional insurance and comprehensive business (rather than holiday) travel and health insurance. Check all the small print in the policy schedules (which, unfortunately, you will only be given after paying the premium), and look out for the important matters — limitations imposed by age, territorial limits and time limits.

Dance UK publishes an information sheet, *A Basic Guide to Insurance*, which is free to members. Equity provide an insurance service, and has arranged a comprehensive Entertainers' Travel Insurance for its members.

The number of incidents of choreographers being sued in the case of accidents is much higher in the USA than the UK. Make sure you are protected by your employers against negligence both in auditions and once dancers have been given a contract to work with you.

*See also:*
**Useful addresses:**
Equity Insurance (booklet)

**Insurance** (page 145)

**Equity** (page 24)

**Dance UK** (page iv)

## 5. Passport

Ensure that your passport is valid with a date of expiry which will permit your return to Britain even if your travel arrangements are delayed or disrupted.

A British Visitor's Passport cannot be used if you intend to work. If you have a BVP, and are visiting for research or personal reasons, check that it will be accepted in the country you will be visiting.

Always keep a separate note of your passport number and other personal details. This will be particularly important in the event of loss, theft or the withholding of your passport by an authority.

If you are travelling abroad with an assistant (who may have a different nationality), check whether he or she has

the necessary passport, visa, work permit, immunisation certificates for entry to the country within which you will be working.

In some countries a hotel or theatre management may require you to lodge your passport with it temporarily. Make sure it is returned as soon as possible.

## 6. Visas and work permits

If you have not already been reliably informed, and if your agent is not already arranging it, you should check with the relevant embassy, high commission or consulate, whether a visa, entry permit, employment permit (or combination of all three) is necessary for the country in which you will be working. A work permit is not necessary for UK citizens to work in countries in the European Economic Area.

If it is the commissioning management or production company which is responsible for obtaining the necessary permits and visas, find out what additional action, if any, you can take to assist them. This might include the preparation of photographs, copies of letters of reference or engagement. It may be your responsibility to set a similar process in motion in the UK.

**The time required for obtaining permits and visas is frequently underestimated. It can take several months for applications to be processed, irrespective of your professional reputation. All applications should be made well in advance.**

Make several copies of any documentation, including photographs, you may have to submit to authorities and which could get lost in the post. Make sure you provide authorities and companies with a reliable postal address and telephone number. You may have to attend a consular office in the UK to have an interview and to have the necessary stamp printed in your passport. This can be done by post, but leave plenty of time.

## 7. Health advice

Information about necessary precautions and immunisations can be obtained from your doctor, health department or travel clinic. Check well in advance which immunisations are required and which are recommended for the country you will be visiting. Some immunisations cannot be given simultaneously and the process of getting immunised may take several weeks. You will need to observe the required sequence of immunisations. Remember to take the certificates abroad with you.

A world-wide, country by country disease and immunisation checklist is available in the booklet *Health Advice for Travellers Anywhere in the World*, published by the Department of Health. This includes information on:

✦ avoiding health risks

✦ planning for healthy travel

✦ obtaining emergency medical treatment

✦ form E111 (which you need to fill out before you travel abroad if you wish to receive free or reduced-cost emergency treatment in most European countries).

If you receive medical treatment abroad and you intend to claim on your medical insurance on returning to Britain, you will need to produce all the associated paperwork—certificates, prescriptions, invoices and receipts as well as the boxes or labels of any medication prescribed.

*See also:*
**Insurance:**
The choreographer as freelance artist (page 148)

**Useful addresses:**
Department of Health (booklet)

**Useful publications:**
Health Advice for Travellers (booklet)

## 8. Translator

You may need to be accompanied by an translator in order to choreograph and direct your work. If this service is necessary, enquire in advance who will pay the translator's fees. Find out whether the translator is sufficiently familiar with all necessary musical, stage, physical and technical vocabulary. Ask when you will be able to meet this person, and for how many hours a day he or she will be with you. Will the translator's time be divided between you and other visiting staff?

If the person providing translation services is not a professional but a member of the commissioning or production company's staff, find out how much time he or she can spend assisting you each day.

If you are told that 'everyone speaks English', it is still sensible to make a few further enquiries.Performers may understand your directions and body language in rehearsal. You may be able to speak enough of the relevant languages to conduct rehearsals. However, you may want to hold an introductory session with some or all of the performers and on this occasion you may need a superior facility with the language since you will need total understanding on the part of the cast. Check the availability of assistance at this sort of meeting or event, as well as for pre- or post-performance 'notes' sessions.

## 9. Public holidays and industrial disputes

Try to get advance information from the host company about the dates of company and public holidays, saints days or local festivals which may slightly reduce your rehearsal period. Find out too what the local tradition is with regard to working on Sundays.

If there is any rumour of an industrial dispute which may affect your work, or a lingering strike affecting the postal services, sea ports, road, rail or air services, try to gain up-to-date information to help make contingency plans.

## 10. Consular advice

In most capital cities, British consular officers are ready to do what they can to help if things go wrong. However, there are limits to the services they can provide. More information about the service can be obtained from the leaflet *Consular Assistance Abroad—Get it Right Before You Go*, available from the Central Office of Information or a local library.

*See also:*
**Useful publications** (booklet)

## 11. Before you go

+ Has your agent and/or solicitor got a telephone or fax contact number and address as well as the dates of your absence?

+ Do you need travellers' cheques, cash or credit card?

+ Is card protection included in your comprehensive insurance?

+ Have you got enough foreign currency (some in small change) to serve your needs until you collect your subsistence?

+ Have you packed a well-stocked first aid kit?

PART 4

PART **4**

Assistants, notators and staff producers

Music

Set and costume design

Lighting design

Videotapes

# Assistants, notators and staff producers

During the course of your career as a choreographer, you may work in collaboration with assistants and other specialists in a variety of settings. This chapter looks at the role of three working relationships you may have, or may need to develop.

## REHEARSAL ASSISTANTS

1. In the professional theatre (dance, opera and plays)

2. With children in theatre and education

## NOTATORS

1. The choreographic score

2. Ownership, security and use

## STAFF PRODUCERS

1. Preparation

2. Rehearsals

3. Performances

4. Revivals

5. Relationship with choreographer

## REHEARSAL ASSISTANTS

### 1. In the professional theatre

Most dance, opera, theatre and film companies employ one or more people who direct or supervise rehearsals. These people may be known as rehearsal director, staff producer, production assistant, dance captain, teacher or notator-repetiteur, amongst other titles. If you are a guest choreographer who would like to build good working relationships within a commissioning company, find out about these people, their job responsibilities, and how they might help you.

Unless you are in a position to bring your own assistant, you may want to ask for a particular assistant from within the company to be available to you or you may want to recommend a person who should be engaged. Discuss whether your assistant will be a freelance with whom you are already familiar, or whether he or she will be assigned to your production from within the staff of the commissioning company. If you are working abroad, ask if the person assigned to you speaks and understands English (if you think there may be a problem). If you bring your own assistant, has it been agreed who will pay the necessary fees, travel and subsistence? Try to discuss your need for an assistant at an early stage, as additional funds will need to be found in the production budget to employ someone in this role. You may have to make a convincing case for the inclusion of an assistant. Consult your agent. At a certain point in your career, you will probably want to ensure that the provision of an assistant is always part of your contract.

If you are not available to oversee your completed work regularly during a season, you may decide to invest in your assistant considerable responsibility for the care and continuing life of one or more works. You will need to be confident that your assistant has a suitable personality and the combination of skills which you feel are important. For example:

✦ musical skills

✦ teaching and coaching skills

✦ organisational ability

✦ some experience of a particular movement tradition which is integral to your choreography

✦ skill in observing, understanding, recording and accurately reconstructing choreography

✦ experience in compiling and delivering pre- or post-performance 'notes'

You will need someone who is reliable and patient, particularly with actors, singers and children; someone whose artistic judgement you trust, and who will keep in touch with you (and your agent if necessary). You may seek a person who will speak for you on occasions and is seen to gain the respect of cast and management. This person should be prepared to work at least some unsociable hours.

If you are not working with someone you already know, try to meet your assistant informally in advance of rehearsals. Discuss in detail areas of responsibility — both creative and practical. Try to define what you expect your assistant to do for you and/or with you:

✦ check and/or prepare schedules

✦ assist in rehearsals

✦ attend to the needs (personal, choreographic, musical) of chorus or specified artists

✦ general coaching and polishing

✦ coach cast changes

✦ teach and coach second casts

✦ attend to actors' movement and staging

✦ attend to children's movement and staging

✦ attend to dancers' movement and staging

✦ record the production in the production book or score

✦ liaise between you and the performers

✦ liaise with other rehearsal-direction staff

✦ liaise with stage management

✦ liaise with accompanists and/or musicians

✦ liaise with chorus manager

✦ give pre- or post-performance 'notes'

✦ attend lighting and technical rehearsals (in addition to other stage calls)

✦ stay and talk after rehearsals

It is also very important to discuss or know in advance how your assistant can work effectively in association with other production assistants, especially those concerned with music, chorus management, voice, text and language.

In the event of a major revival which you are not able to undertake without

assistance, or a transfer of your work to a different company in the UK or abroad, it is worth remembering to reserve time in which to consult your assistant, or other guardian of your work, as he or she may have a significant practical contribution to make, particularly at the preparation and time-tabling stage of negotiations.

*Much of the substance of this guide is built upon the experiences of assistant choreographers and assistants to choreographers and directors. If, by agreement, your assistant has major, even sole responsibility for the re-staging of one of your choreographic works, in the UK or abroad, make sure he or she has a copy of the guide. He or she will be making a variety of plans and decisions on your behalf and may welcome the **checklists** of matters to be considered.*

*See also:*
**Working as a choreographer** (page 31)

**Child performance regulations** (page 162)

**Working as a choreographer in opera and musical theatre** (page 53)

**Working as a choreographer for a play** (page 62)

## 2. With children in theatre and education

These notes relate to aspects of rehearsal assistance with professional or amateur productions with children who may or may not have a particular form of dance training or experience.

If you are going to be working on a large scale, with a large number of children or young people, your task will be eased by having an assistant or children's manager. When you have enough information to assess the nature of the forthcoming project, discuss the possibility of employing an assistant—or several assistants—with your employer. Illustrate the ways in which your assistant(s) could affect the success, standards, efficiency and safety of the whole venture from first rehearsal through to the last performance.

A fully professional production which includes children will almost certainly require a trained children's manager to be responsible for the licensing and management of the children who take part.

If there are budgetary limitations (especially in community and educational work) on the inclusion of an assistant in the production team, investigate the possibility of enlisting the help and support of a member of staff from the children's school or college, or a parent or guardian with the necessary skills. Either may be prepared to help you without payment. See if you can secure a contribution towards the parent's expenses. In an ideal setting, your parent-helper will enlist a colleague to help him or her and the level of assistance will increase to your advantage.

Try to find time to discover your assistant's qualifications or areas of interest or speciality. Is it important that your assistant can drive, and holds a clean driving licence? You may discover dance, music, design, sport, language, history, cultural studies or first aid skills in a previously unknown volunteer. Your helper may have much to contribute and will probably know the children better than you.

Working as an assistant can be a rewarding experience for adults (qualified or unqualified) of all ages, learning new skills and giving of their own. Will it be necessary to teach or guide a relatively inexperienced assistant during the rehearsal period? The assistant may be assigned to you as part of work experience or vocational training and may need guidance in areas such as reading music, recording choreography, operating a video camera, making schedules and 'crowd control'.

Once you have found a suitable helper for your work, try to find time to discuss areas of responsibility and methods of communication within your busy schedule. Decide where you can leave notes for each other, for example, and find out whether you can telephone each other at night or in the early morning.

Working as an assistant should be accorded due respect and recognised as an invaluable part of vocational training which may lead to the development of full-time or freelance employment as an assistant to one or various choreographers, or to work as a choreographer.

*See also:*
**Child performance regulations** (page 162)

**Working as a choreographer in the community** (page 92)

**Insurance** (page 145)

**Health and safety** (page 156)

**Working as a choreographer with schools and youth organisations** (page 85)

## NOTATORS

These notes, written in the context of United Kingdom legislation and practice, aim to draw attention to a few of the implications and advantages for the choreographer and his or her work if a comprehensive and accurate movement notation system is a component of the production.

If you are not familiar with the ways in which collaboration with a notator (using the Benesh or Laban systems of movement notation) can serve you and your work, you could begin your enquiries by contacting the Benesh Institute and/or the Labanotation Institute. These organisations are the representative bodies in the UK for the two movement notation systems which you are most likely to meet in day-to-day usage in the world of western and non-western dance, dance-theatre, opera and film work, African and South Asian dance, and in schools and universities.

*See also:*
**Useful addresses** (booklet)

Some dance company managements employ qualified professional notators (also known as choreologists) on a permanent contract. Other organisations engage notators on a freelance basis according to the needs of the research project or theatrical production. Some notators are also repetiteurs, rehearsal directors, reconstructors or choreographers' personal assistants. Representatives from company managements, and experienced practitioners of the notation systems may be willing to offer informal advice on the short- and long-term employment of notators and the value of notation to a choreographer.

The advantages of movement notation to a dance or theatre company are many. For example, a day-to-day record of the choreography in progress can be invaluable to choreographers, directors and performers alike. Notated works which have not been included in a company repertory for a period can be revived accurately and efficiently, recapturing the original spirit of the choreography. Subject to the necessary permissions and correct procedures, a movement score can be transmitted to another company and country in advance of a busy choreographer's arrival (or that of his or her approved assistant) for reconstruction by a qualified resident notator, thereby saving time and expense.

As a guest choreographer you may want to check in advance on the notator's exclusive availability for your rehearsals. A resident company notator may have various scheduled responsibilities for existing productions in the repertory of the commissioning company, and it may not be possible for all his or her time to be given to record your work.

## 1. The choreographic score

Generally speaking, the compilation of a complete movement score evolves in at least two stages from the drafting of a preliminary or working score during rehearsals to the writing of a 'final' or master score (which may acquire additions after the first series of performances). The time required to compile a detailed movement score depends on the working methods of the choreographer and notator, the choreographer's movement 'style', the size of the cast, the nature and scale of the production to be notated, and a host of surrounding or interwoven details.

A comprehensive master score is a sophisticated record of the choreography and its integration with music or sound source, set and costume design, props, libretto or text, multi-level staging, and special effects amongst other things. As a future source of reference, especially for the choreographer and others who may not be able to read the notation, additional information within the movement score should not be overlooked. Some notators will include reference to a choreographer's research material, or record selected dramatic or production comments made by a choreographer to the notator and/or cast while creating the work. Also included might be; useful diagrams, stage ground-plans, detailed production credits, timings of movement sequences or acts and a variety of longhand notes. All this information offers valuable practical assistance in the event of a revival or adaptation of the choreography.

Although you are unlikely to want any cuts or alterations to be made to your choreography without your permission, you should discuss with the rehearsal staff and/or the notator any minor adjustments which you would find acceptable if it were necessary for them to adapt the choreography on tour for different spaces. These should be notated and, if possible, rehearsed.

You may want to encourage degrees of individuality in the performance of a movement style. You may want to alter your choreography to some extent from time to time. You may be keen to preserve more than one version of a whole work, scene or sequence. It will be valuable for all concerned if you make clear any consequent requirement for the notator to augment the movement score to reflect your wishes, thereby keeping the record accurate, relevant and 'alive'.

Several choreographers and notators working in dance, opera and musical theatre productions have referred to the practical value of notated curtain calls to complete the record of the production. These might be carefully choreographed, sometimes in stylised form and accompanied by music, and may involve a large number of people in defined groups. This part of the production has a structure, pace and flavour which the choreographer intends to be respected and maintained, even if it is subject to some variation from time to time. Its choreographic detail is seldom adequately recorded in longhand by stage management or producers' assistants, though their records may contribute to the reconstruction process.

## 2. Ownership, security and use

It is essential to establish the ownership of a movement score—the manuscript itself. If, by contract, you own the copyright in the choreography, ideally you should make sure you own and possess the manuscript as well. However, it is common practice for a theatre or management to insist upon ownership of that score if they paid for it to be written. In this event you should reach agreement with the management as to how the score is to be used.

If an organisation requests that your choreographic work should be notated (for its practical and archival benefit), and it has never previously been recorded by being 'fixed' in writing (such as movement notation) or by any other means (such as film or video), the choreographer's copyright as 'author' will be established. In this case the 'author' is the choreographer not the notator (but the notator's authorship of the score itself may be a secondary copyright). If you agree to the recording of your work in movement notation, put that consent in writing. All parties, such as the commissioner of the score and the notator, should have a copy of this written consent. Similar written consent should be given if you are using your own notator hired at your own expense.

Discuss or find out about the secure location and storage conditions for the working and master score of your choreographic work. As a precaution against loss of all authorised copies of the score in one disaster, it is advisable to encourage the safekeeping of the master score in separate housing from any working copies. It has been the practice of many choreographers and companies to register choreographic scores with the Benesh Institute Library for copyright and security purposes.

Subject to your agreement, video recordings of your work may be used in conjunction with the score by the notator for educational, teaching or revival purposes. Despite the fact that it is an independent visual record of one rehearsal or performance of your work, the video will tend to be treated by future casts, research students and historians as the definitive record. It is therefore increasingly important to share with your notator your thoughts on the video's accuracy and merits. Ask your notator to record these in writing, or attach your own commentary to the video itself.

*See also:*

**Copyright** (page 151)

**Videotapes:** Labelling (page 140)
Storing (page 141)

**Working as a choreographer:**
Transfers: consultation with the production team (page 49)

## STAFF PRODUCERS

Freelance choreographers are required to work effectively within various artistic staff structures. This profile of an opera staff producer in the UK may serve to introduce a choreographer to this key role in the life of an opera, operetta, musical theatre work, masque or play both here and abroad. In other countries the job title and definition of duties may vary a little from those described here.

A resident staff producer (or 'staff director') is the producer/director's assistant. He or she differs from a freelance assistant director in that he or she is under contract to a company rather than to one specific production. In the long-term, his or her knowledge of the repertory, resident and visiting artists, personnel and working practices of the company will provide substantial support to a visiting director, producer or choreographer—a foundation that a freelance assistant may not necessarily have.

In some companies, a staff producer must have a working knowledge of (typically) French, German and Italian, and may be fluent in all three and more languages. He or she will have considerable knowledge of music and theatre as well as good organisational skills.

## 1. Preparation

Before opera production rehearsals begin, a staff producer will acquaint himself with the opera, its history, music and libretto. He or she may be closely involved in the auditioning of actors, dancers, children, and will advise the resident or guest producer how best to use the limited number of rehearsal sessions available according to the terms and conditions of the performers' contracts. A staff producer may be working on overlapping productions. He or she will regularly draw up and/or check the weekly schedule in consultation with other staff from its draft form through to its final state prior to distribution. In an opera company operating a repertory system, the efficient construction of a complex weekly schedule may require the staff producer to liaise with the company manager, other staff producers, chorus manager, music staff, choreographers, children's manager, stage management, designer and lighting designer, fight director and wardrobe. He or she may need to consult other schedules such as advance or technical ones, as well as information regarding cast arrival dates, agreed cast absences (non-availability or 'n/a's') or cast involvement in other productions and availability of the conductor or deputy. He or she may also know to what extent (if at all) the production budget could sustain the inclusion of limited 'extra' sessions if required.

## 2. Rehearsals

A staff producer will make a detailed written record of the production in an interleaved copy of the music score. The production score will be of immediate practical use and will also be used for revival purposes in association with any video recordings, photographs, stage management score or choreographic score. The staff producer, with an assistant on large productions, may 'organise' chorus movement and staging and actors' movement and staging with,

or independently of, the choreographer. He or she will communicate with all performers, stage management, chorus master and accompanist — thereby relieving the producer/director of many organisational tasks. He or she will also be involved with technical rehearsals, and will rehearse understudies ('covers') of all ranks, as well as scheduled and unscheduled replacement casts.

## 3. Performances

As members of the creative production team may have dispersed shortly after the first performance, a staff producer will be on duty to observe from the auditorium and monitor standards of performance and cast changes. He or she will give notes to performers and liaise closely with technical, production and stage management staff and may remain responsible for the production for many months or years.

## 4. Revivals

The availability of the original producer/ director of a production may determine whether the original staff producer will assist or direct the revival of the opera after its absence from the repertory for some months or years. That staff producer might also direct the transfer or tour of the opera to another country. His or her knowledge of the production is likely to help in thorough preparation and the company's capacity to achieve a swift, newly-cast staging, often constrained by limited budget and time.

## 5. Relationship with choreographer

As a regular or new guest choreographer in an opera company, an understanding of the nature and extent of the staff producer's job, and a good working relationship with him or her is extremely important. That relationship will be enhanced if the staff producer has some knowledge of and respect for the world of dance, dancers and choreographers. Try to meet in advance of rehearsals, particularly if you have not worked together before. If the staff producer does not already know how your choreography is expected to integrate with the production, explain your ideas and plans, and discuss what you can expect from each other in terms of practical and creative support.

A staff producer can often be regarded as a facilitator. He or she may at times act as a bridge or messenger between you and the producer/director, especially if you are working in separate studios. It will also be productive if, when working on new productions, revivals or re-stagings abroad, your approved assistant or notator-assistant and the staff producer gain mutual confidence and respect. Their production notes or scores are likely to be of mutual assistance, and they may have overlapping tasks and responsibilities whilst working in the partial or total absence of the producer/ director or choreographer.

*See also:*
**Working as a choreographer in opera and musical theatre** (page 53)
**Child performance regulations** (page 162)

**Working as a choreographer:**
Casting (page 39)
Transfers: consultation with the production team (page 49)

# Music

Whether music is a source for the choreographic ideas, or a means to articulate what a choreographer already has in mind, its function needs to be carefully considered, as does the choice between making use of already composed music or having music commissioned and composed for the purpose. The following practical advice is intended to help guide you towards the successful presentation of dance with music, by identifying and suggesting ways of resolving the problems most commonly encountered. The advice is applicable to choreographers wanting to collaborate with, or use the music of, song-writers and composers whose work is contemporary, classical or popular.

1. The use of live and recorded music in public

2. Commissioned music

3. Working with conductors or musical directors

4. Scores and tapes

5. Rehearsal musicians

6. Programme and publicity credits for music

7. Learning more about music

8. The Musicians' Union

## 1. The use of live and recorded music in public

If you plan to present dance performances at venues in the UK accompanied by live or recorded music you **must seek and have in writing** the correct permissions and licences. Clearances and permissions are normally the responsibility of the management. If you are working outside the structure of a company, take expert advice, perhaps through one of these organisations:

**PRS:** Performing Right Society Ltd
**MCPS:** Mechanical Copyright Protection Society
**PPL:** Phonographic Performance Ltd
**Patent Office,** Department of Trade and Industry

*See also:*
**Useful addresses** (booklet)

Copyright ownership of musical works may belong to composers, the executors of a dead composer's estate, publishers and/or recording companies. **You may not perform or allow the performance of any copyright music in public without the permission of the copyright owner.** 'In public' means anywhere outside your domestic circle. Performances in clubs, hotels, restaurants, factories, are 'public' even if the audience is limited to club members or employees of the venue. The venue must have a licence for the performance of copyright music on its premises, and obtaining permission from the composer and publisher and any other relevant bodies for the use of music in public dance performance may attract certain costs which must be identified when you start negotiations.

The fact that you possess a record, tape, compact disc or printed sheet music of a work you want to use does not give you the right to perform that music in public. You should also be aware that, in addition to the composer's copyright, there is also a separate copyright in the sound recording of any recorded music. This usually belongs to the recording company.

Some specific uses of copyright music are permitted without the owner's permission. These include research and private study, and performances given in an educational establishment where the audience is composed of students and teaching staff. It is advisable to check with the publishers, PPL or PRS, as there are other exemptions with particular provisions.

Some composers do not want their music performed in association with dance or in conjunction with any theatrical production. No persuasion or negotiation is possible. The composer's publisher or the executor of a composer's estate must continue to uphold this condition in accordance with the composer's wishes.

Much music in public demand is in copyright which lasts for the composer's lifetime and, since July 1995, for 70 years after his or her death for composers published in the European Community. This act means that composers protected by the previous 50-year period whose works were out of copyright will return into copyright as the law will be applied retrospectively: for instance, Elgar, Holst and Delius, who all died in 1934, Respighi in 1936, Ravel in 1937 and Rachmaninov in 1943, but not Gershwin (who died in 1937), whose works were American, not European, publications in origin.

If you plan to tour abroad the licensing authorities (PRS, MCPS, PPL) will advise you about regulations which may apply in each country. Leave plenty of time for investigations, and time for problems to be resolved, before you leave this country.

Also bear in mind that international copyright regulations are varied and complex. To avoid any breach of rights you are advised to take expert advice, such as from the publisher or PRS.

In making use of an existing composition, whether commissioned or not, you have a legal obligation to contact the composer to gain permission if you want to make changes to the work's structure and duration. If the work is divided into sections, the order of these should not be changed without the permission of the composer or publisher. However, when choreographing to the music of a composer whose works are in the public domain (out of copyright) there might be occasions when you request an alteration to the order originally specified by the composer. Unless there is prior agreement with a composer, you should not end or fade out a recorded work arbitrarily if your choreography does not match its length.

It is very important to be aware of the risks involved if you ignore the proper procedures with regard to music rights. A recording company or publisher could charge a retrospective and very high fee by way of a penalty. These bodies would also be within their rights to stop your performances.

Publishers, record companies and the licensing authorities will give advice and quotations at any stage. Organisations such as PRS, MCPS and PPL, and the Department of Trade and Industry (ask for 'copyright enquiries') publish advisory leaflets (often free) upon request. You should not encounter difficulties if you follow the procedures described in the next section.

*See also:*
**Copyright** (page 151)

**Useful addresses** (booklet)

## *Choreography to live music*

✦ Approach the publisher for a licence for permission to use the music for choreographic purposes. It is helpful to give as much information as possible about the number of performances planned, the seating capacity of the theatres or venues to be visited, and the ticket prices.

✦ If the composer of the music you wish to use does not have a publisher, approach him or her directly. Secure any agreement in writing.

✦ Check that the theatre has a PRS licence for live music. Give details of the style of dance you are using (contemporary, jazz, tap and so on). A PRS licence is not always required.

✦ Check the size of the ensemble needed and the costs of the players.

## *Choreography to a complete bought commercial recording*

✦ Approach the publisher for a licence (which includes permission for the choreography and agreement for performing fees). Give as much information as possible about the number of performances planned, the seating capacity of the theatres or venues to be visited, and the ticket prices.

✦ Check that the theatre has a PRS licence for the use of recorded music. Give details of the style of dance you are using (contemporary, jazz, tap and so on). A PRS licence is not always required.

✦ With details of the original commercial tape or CD you wish to use, approach the PPL'S General Licensing Department which will license the performance using that recording. This covers permission from the record company.

✦ Enquire whether your employer or producing company has any agreement with the Musicians' Union concerning the use of recorded music.

Dance companies which are members of the Theatrical Management Association (TMA) are party to an agreement with the Musicians' Union under which the Union's permission has to be sought to use recorded music to accompany live performance. The dance company needs to apply well in advance of the request to use the taped music giving its reasons for needing a recording rather than using live musicians. Permission is given on artistic grounds, but not if it is a matter of finance. Each case is judged on its own merits. While dance companies which are not members of the TMA are not party to this agreement, the same conditions may still apply.

*Choreography to a performance tape made from a commercial recording*

✦ Approach the publisher for a licence (which includes permission for the choreography and agreement for performing fees). It is helpful to give as much information as possible about the number of performances planned, the seating capacity of the theatres or venues to be visited, and the ticket prices.

✦ Inform the publisher of any cuts or additions made to the music.

✦ Check that the theatre has a PRS licence for the use of recorded music. Give details of the style of dance you are using (contemporary, jazz, tap and so on). A PRS licence is not always required.

✦ Approach MCPS for a licence to make the tape, and the record company for permission (if in doubt, contact PPL who will advise you on this matter).

✦ Enquire whether your employer or producing company has any agreement with the Musicians' Union concerning the use of recorded music.

Any transference of a recording from a commercial record to any other medium (including tape) is automatically a breach of the 'Performers' Right' and, as such, permission should be sought from the Musicians' Union.

It is advisable to keep safely copies of all correspondence, letters of agreement, licences, invoices and receipts for charges. Check the dates and terms of any agreements. Send each organisation a copy of any relevant correspondence or agreement you have made with another relevant party.

## 2. Commissioned music

Commission fees are paid to the composer for the act of composing a piece of music. However, there may be extra charges (normally made by the composer's publisher) for the preparation of scores and 'performing materials'—for instance, conductor's score, orchestral parts, vocal scores and tapes—and for the hire or sale of the performing materials. A rehearsal or piano-reduction score or tape is a requirement usually specific to dance works, so make it clear from the start if this will be needed. These additional costs must be specified and allowed for in the music budget before the commission is undertaken.

The exact size and instrumental composition of the orchestra or ensemble which will play the music should be established as soon as possible in the negotiations. The composer or arranger should be informed if there are any necessary limitations on numbers of players.

Whatever the scale of the musical composition it is very important to establish the completion and delivery dates for the composer's work and the orchestral parts. This could be many months or years in advance of your choreographic work, or could be simultaneous with your work in certain circumstances. If a composition is not finished as planned before the physical choreographic process begins, you may have to start working without music or with limited taped sections. Be aware that composers and choreographers have different working methods, especially with regard to the structure of a work which may only emerge choreographically as the dance movement develops, but which is usually well-defined musically in the composer's mind at an early stage.

Several composers who regularly write for dance have drawn attention to a situation that can develop when, after the music is composed and accepted and the choreography put into rehearsal for some weeks, the choreographer suddenly finds the need for an extra minute of music or a new linking phrase, to facilitate an awkward scene-change or something similar affecting entries and exits. It may be impossible (or much more complicated than the choreographer imagines) for the composer to integrate extra music at such a late stage. Although a composer may be willing to try to assist the choreographer with a predicament which may not be entirely the fault of the choreographer, sufficient time must be allowed for the composer to accomplish the extra work, and the choreographer should be aware of any consequential expense.

If a composer makes a choreographer a rehearsal tape of, for example, a string quartet, and makes this on a synthesiser, this may save money by avoiding a recording session, but the tape will produce an inflexible rhythm and tempo with no 'give and take' in the manner of playing. Moreover, the tone quality may be thought inferior to the 'live' instrumental sound, and when you come to rehearsal with the live ensemble the sound may be disconcertingly different. Weigh up the relative costs and advantages of a live session with musicians or musicians imitated by a synthesiser.

Keep in mind that recording session costs will involve fees to the players, the cost of the studio (which may or may not include the services of a sound engineer), mixing sessions and a fee to the composer if he or she is directing the session. (See advice on the Musicians' Union later in this chapter.)

Try to attend as many rehearsals of the commissioned music as possible. Encourage the dancers and any other relevant performers to attend as well. Encourage the composer to attend as many of your choreographic rehearsals as possible.

When your production has reached a stage at which live music and dance are rehearsed together, take full advantage of the limited time you will have to listen and rehearse to the full sound. The use of musicians is expensive. You will rarely have the amount of live (as opposed to tape) rehearsal that you would like. Choreographers should also be aware that combined music and dance rehearsals provide a precious and limited opportunity for the composer (who may or may not be the conductor or ensemble leader) to attend to final musical detail and hear the work in an orchestra pit or staged setting. Although it may appear to be an opportunity for your further collaboration, in practice both the composer and conductor's prime focus may temporarily be on the music, musicians or singers and not on the choreography.

### 3. Working with conductors or musical directors

Find out whether the music, commissioned or otherwise, will be conducted by a resident or guest conductor or by the composer. The choreographer should be satisfied that the conductor and/or composer will attend a sufficient number of studio and stage rehearsals to facilitate adequate discussion about all aspects of the musical integration and presentation.

Whether you are working on a new production, a revival, charity gala or a transfer from one country to another, arrange a meeting with the conductor, musical director or their deputies if relevant. They may have advice to contribute at an early stage in the preparations. Conversely, they may know remarkably little of the proposed or existing movement content in a production and may be interested to discover your plans. Try to build on any initial professional acquaintance with conductors, rehearsal accompanists, chorus masters and language coaches. The conductor, particularly, will expect to be treated with a great deal of respect. The opportunities for relaxed discussion may be limited but try to be articulate about your aims, ideas and approach including the practicalities. This could be mutually productive, especially if you are arranging or re-staging movement on a large scale which includes, for instance, dancers, singers, actors and children.

In international opera houses it is not unusual for a conductor to join a production at a comparatively late stage in the rehearsal period. Much depends on the conductor's over-all commitment and general interest and his or her availability. Some conductors are reluctant to attend studio rehearsals devoted exclusively to dance or stylised movement, whereas they will attend studio rehearsals which include singers and other performers. The conductor may consider the choreography of little importance; there may be a rehearsal schedule with clashing demands; there may be no deputy to enable him or her to attend any of your rehearsals.

If using a concert work do not impose too rigid a rhythm or tempo (speed) on music that may need to 'breathe' with flexibility of phrasing, and which can affect the dancers' phrasing in consequence. Do not rely on recordings in the matter of setting tempi, but always discuss them with the conductor, musical director or, when working with a soloist, small band or trio for example, with the instrumentalists concerned. The dancers in turn should be alerted to any significant differences in tempo taken by an assistant or deputy conductor. Matters of tempo would ideally be discussed early in the rehearsal period, perhaps even before starting to choreograph, and some flexibility in approach is required from all parties if problems are to be avoided. If you have a disagreement at any stage in the collaboration you should be able to speak from a standpoint of real knowledge, so it is always advisable to do your homework on the music and know in detail how the music plays.

If at any time you have a comment concerning the sound or location of a particular musical instrument or musician, do this through the conductor, where there is one, or the leader of the instrumental ensemble.

When an opera or dance production has reached its final staging rehearsals there will very often be little or no time allowed for the choreographer and/or the producer to make any substantial choreographic adjustments which are felt to be necessary. The emphasis at this stage is on voices, diction, quality of sound from all participants and orchestral balance, sometimes at the initial expense of the choreography. At this stage final decisions and the direction of the combined artistic forces tend to be the prerogative of the conductor, though much will depend on the strength, harmony, and flexibility of the working relationships within the creative production team.

## 4. Scores and tapes

A reduced orchestral score prepared for a variety of rehearsal purposes is often known as a piano-reduction score, short score or vocal score (if sung text and vocal parts are included). These scores are sometimes more portable and easier to follow than the full score. They will not, however, indicate the full range of instruments in the full score, nor will they present the complete 'sound colour' or 'texture' found in a recording or live performance of that work. Make sure that you and the dancers are familiar with the full instrumentation and sound.

It is essential to check that any piano-reduction score, full score or rehearsal recordings you have bought or have been given meet with the approval of the composer, conductor or musical director in order to avoid wasting time with the 'wrong' editions, orchestrations, or versions of the music or text. Two published scores which at first glance appear to be the same, but have slightly different covers, should be checked through very carefully, page by page. If cuts or additions to a score have been approved by all relevant parties, make sure **your** scores or recordings also include these amendments.

Where musicians who are members of the Musicians' Union are to be involved in the performance, and these musicians are requested to make a recording in advance for use as a rehearsal tape, the agreement of the Musicians' Union is required prior to its manufacture.

Choreographers creating work to choral music, and choreographers working in opera and musical theatre, may come across 'S A T B' in scores and on rehearsal schedules. This abbreviation refers to soprano, alto, tenor and bass. You could encounter 'T A T B' in connection with church or cathedral music. This refers to treble (boy soprano), alto, tenor and bass.

If 'period' instruments for 'early music' (usually before the mid-eighteenth century) are involved, remember that some stringed instruments can go out of tune quickly and some re-tuning may be needed during an evening's production. A tape of music played by period instruments may have its volume boosted in the rehearsal studio, and the same sound live on stage or from the pit can sound quiet by comparison, and perhaps not fully audible to the performers on stage. You will need then to consult the sound engineer, who will be as keen as you to get the quality and balance right, perhaps by some form of amplification of the sound on stage. It helps if you can discuss this in the right technical language.

## 5. Rehearsal musicians

Try to ensure that your rehearsal accompanist has all the music needed, and that this is clearly marked if any cuts have been make, or repetitions left out. Your accompanist will want to have the music in his or her possession with adequate time for preparation, especially if the work is known to be complicated. To avoid possible embarrassment and consequent delay, and if you have reason to anticipate difficulties, ask for a skilled pianist to be available to tackle a complex score. It is always an advantage if your rehearsals are supported by an accompanist who understands the music, any text involved, and your ideas about its place in your conception for the choreography.

Discuss at the outset the best, draught-free locations for musicians and their instruments, whether keyboard or hand-held, with adequate lighting, and whether playing from chairs or seated on the floor. Remember that your accompanist will need breaks during the rehearsal day no less than the dancers.

In collaboration with the composer or accompanist, and your assistant if you have one, establish useful and clear 'counts', well-defined musical, choreographic or vocal phrases, or sections which can be marked on the score as starting and stopping places for rehearsal purposes. Be aware of the needs and response of the performers in this task, especially where there may be patterns of so-called 'dancers' counts' or phrases which differ from the musical phrases notated in the score.

## 6. Programme and publicity credits for music

Whether the composer is alive, or no longer living, you may like to consider some of the following points. Even if you are working in a company with press and publications departments, acknowledgements to music and musicians need to be checked.

◆ Check the spelling of the composer's name and exactly how it should appear. If in doubt, contact the composer's agent, publisher or executor.

◆ Check the title of the composition and its spelling, and exactly how it should appear.

◆ If a foreign title, discuss giving it a translation.

◆ Always identify the composition by name (especially if different from the dance work) and opus number, if any, with basic instrumentation (for instance, 'for strings' or 'for two voices and tape'); possibly identify the titles of the musical 'movements' or sections.

✦ If a small ensemble (trio, sextet), give the names of the players and the instrument each performs.

✦ Consider whether the origin of the music should be explained in a short programme-note, and who should provide it.

✦ Unless there is a composer's biography printed elsewhere in the programme, you should give his or her years of birth and death, and possibly nationality.

✦ There may be an obligation to acknowledge that music is used 'by kind permission of...' the publisher and/or recording company. Check this with one or both of these, and obtain the exact form of words.

✦ Special acknowledgements may be expected (or required) to the commissioner, funding body or sponsor of the composition. You might also have to mention the name of any dedicatee. If this is a condition, consult the sponsor or publisher about the exact wording of the credit and the placing of any logo.

✦ As an extra courtesy, send the composer copies of any reviews following the first performance.

## 7. Learning more about music

While a knowledge of musical theory is not a prerequisite for successful collaboration with a composer, some technical education will deepen your musical appreciation and enable you to communicate with musicians more clearly and in their language. It will be an advantage if you know how to read a musical score and find your way around it with ease, although even the most experienced choreographer may need guidance to understand the lay-out of complex scores.

Do not be afraid to admit to a lack of technical knowledge in any dialogue with a composer, conductor or any member of the musical team. Any use of inappropriate musical terminology on your part will be quickly noticed and may be confusing. It is worth keeping in mind that some words common in dance parlance, such as 'dynamics', 'texture', 'line', will probably have a different meaning and usage for musicians, so you should always clarify your meaning in any discussion.

If you want to know how to read a musical score, and learn more about the terms, signs, symbols and forms in the language of music, join an evening or further education class, or find a musician to help you with some regular tuition. Look out for weekend or longer courses devoted to the collaboration between choreographers and composers. Well-known publishers produce reasonably priced and concise guides to the rudiments and theory of music, with an approach to musical analysis. A good dictionary of music will always be a useful piece of equipment. Go to a range of musical events to help learn to recognise the sound, quality and texture of diverse music and musical instruments.

## 8. The Musicians' Union

If you are working without the support of expert management, you should be aware that the booking of musicians to rehearse and perform must be in accordance with Musicians' Union rates and conditions.

The Musicians' Union's general policies include seeking to improve the status and remuneration of musicians and protecting both the statutory and contractual rights of its members. Where appropriate, the MU makes national agreements for each type of employment a musician is offered. It makes representations to the government on a wide range of matters including copyright, arts policy and funding, broadcasting policy, work permits for foreign musicians, and responds to all new legislation likely to affect musicians.

The MU, aware of current rapid technological change, seeks to ensure that members obtain a fair return for the increasing uses that are made of their performances, particularly in the audio-visual field, film, television, cable and video.

MU rates are re-negotiated at regular intervals, so it is advisable to keep in touch with the organisation for current details, which are always available upon request. Rates and session lengths depend on the place where your work is being presented and whether it is an amateur, West End or regional venue. Television work and recording sessions have a different set of rates again.

*See also:*

**Copyright** (page 151)

**Working as a choreographer** (page 31)

**Working as a choreographer in opera and musical theatre** (page 53)

**Contract** (page 3)

**Working as a choreographer for film** (page 67)

# Set and costume design

One of the most important decisions you will make when assembling ideas for new choreography is the choice of a designer or team of designers. The nature and scale of your design team will depend on your production budget and the importance you place on design. Some choreographers design the sets, lighting and costumes for their choreography. This chapter addresses those who do not. Its purpose is to highlight some practical aspects of the collaborative process which require special attention, especially if the designer is relatively unfamiliar with the special needs of choreographers and performers who move expansively. The design matters discussed here are those that choreographers, management, dancers and other performers most frequently find problematic—for example, floor surfaces and footwear.

The chapter refers to a choreographer's work in dance, opera, musical theatre, plays and film, and is applicable both on a small and large scale.

1. Discussions with the designer

2. The model

3. Costume considerations

4. Items for rehearsal—checklist

5. Floor surfaces

6. Footwear

> A highly-experienced designer commented shortly before the première of a nineteenth century opera with two very famous extended dance sequences; 'If I'd known there was going to be so much dancing I'd have reduced the rake and given you a larger space.' Nice to know at this late stage in the production schedule!
>
> Kate Flatt, choreographer

## 1. Discussions with the designer

It is very important to know that you and your chosen design team are 'talking the same language', and that the design brief is clear, however simple or complex the end result is intended to be. Any special requirements you have must be clearly articulated from the start.

Following an invitation or commission to create a work, a management will want to know how many people will be involved in the design. Will there be one person designing lighting, costumes and set or a different specialist for each element? You and your designer(s) will be required to present your ideas very clearly, and a management will be keen to see all the elements (scenery, furniture, costumes, props, masks) delivered on time and within the design budget. Late delivery is likely to lead to further expense. If changes to the original plans are necessary, they must be made with sufficient time to complete without compromise to the production and, ideally, within the scope of the budget. Some managements may be able and willing to accommodate limited alterations to original ideas. Much will depend

on the relationship between choreographer, designer and management, as well as on their individual experience, working methods, the scale of the production, the budget and the time available. Make sure that you and your designer or design team is aware of the amount of money there is to spend.

Have you allocated sufficient time for full discussions with your designer? Discussions may be months or even years in advance of your first rehearsal, depending on the nature, scale and budget of the production. You may wish to schedule a series of meetings, informal or formal, with your designer(s), arrange to see their design work and welcome them to attend rehearsals of your current choreography.

There may be circumstances in which a design element or choreographic matter remains unresolved or undefined following extensive discussion. It is important in these circumstances to feel mutually confident of a solution and to know your time limits. In these cases it is very important to keep the management informed of your progress.

The preferred working method of a designer may mean that, although preliminary discussion has taken place, the refinement of the design ideas takes final shape during the rehearsal period when the designer is able to see both you and the dancers in action. Managements are not fond of this method, but it may be built into the contract of an experienced designer.

If you are planning choreography for a large-scale production—perhaps two or three acts—you and the designer should study the cast 'breakdown' (a list of cast involved, scene by scene, with details of their character roles). You will want to make choreographic and design decisions about small groups or ensembles, corps de ballet, chorus, children, quick changes and the provision of costumes for each alternative cast.

If it is anticipated that any of your choreographic work will tour, you should discuss with management and the design team any adaptation from the original design which may be necessary for the work's presentation in a variety of different venues. It is important that both choreographer and designer have plans and elevations of touring venues early on, since the size of the get-in and the limitations of various stages or performing spaces can radically affect the design. You may also need to discuss transport and make sure there is sufficient technical help at each venue.

A choreographer may be invited to create fresh choreography to accompany the existing sets and costumes of a production following a period of absence from a company's repertory. In this case you should consider many aspects of the commission before signing a contract, especially the subject of design. At the very least you may want to try to see a video of the production as it used to be. Try to arrange access to the sets if at all possible. There may be detailed design plans and production photographs available for you to study. Try to see the costumes. Arrange to meet the original designer and assess whether you can work together effectively. Discuss the possible inclusion of new costumes, replacements or any refurbishments which may be possible within the design budget.

If you have been invited to join a creative production team long after the engagement of other personnel, you will need to see the designs and to meet the designer. Try to see the model of the set, props and all relevant costumes as soon as possible. This may mean seeing the costumes in an incomplete state. You will need to know how much space there is for dance or stylised movement as well as the location of all entrances and exits, trap doors, ramps, staircases, balconies, anterooms and how any mechanical, flying or hydraulic devices work. You may need to know if quick costume changes are possible at the side of or under the stage. How versatile are certain props, items of furniture, scaffolding and other structures? Find the right person to help you in each case; artistic director, production manager, technical director, head of design, costume department, props department or model maker.

## 2. The model

This is a meticulously constructed scale model of the set. It includes fixed or suspended structures within the performing space (proscenium or other). As soon as you can, study the model and ask the designer or assistant as much as possible about the integral features and how they function. You may have questions about, for instance, masking, access to entrances, the gradient of raked staging or ramps, the location of cloths and gauzes, split level staging, revolves, flown features, mechanical devices or scenic projections. Any of these design elements might affect your choreographic planning.

Talk to the lighting designer, as his or her requirements for off-stage space will not be shown on the model and may have direct relevance to your choreographic plans.

*See also:* **Lighting design** (page 136)

When model and costume designs created in the UK are presented to a company abroad, the model remains there to be available to the local technical and design team who will build the set and make the costumes. It is therefore important to make sure that, after a visit, you have sufficient documentation of the details of design to bring back to the UK, if you are not preparing the choreography on location. It should be the commissioning company's responsibility to prepare these materials for you, preferably clear colour photographs.

## 3. Costume considerations

The form and method of presentation for costume design will vary from designer to designer. Detailed, painted drawings may be offered, or impressionistic sketches with swatches of fabric or colour attached. You should ask for further explanation if some aspects of the drawing or design require more detail. If it is not immediately apparent, try to understand how the costume 'works'; how it clings, stretches, hangs or moves; the nature, quality and weight of the fabric which will be used; whether the weight of the fabric will bring problems of balance to a performer; or whether its texture may be unpleasant or unsafe for the wearer and anyone partnering the wearer.

Try to make opportunities to see costumes in the construction stages. This will help you to understand the function, dimension, construction and effect of integral features (for instance, wigs, wings, large headpieces, britches, voluminous underskirts, hoops, panniers, farthingales or bustles) and to know how much space the fully-costumed figure occupies. A rehearsal version of any

unusual costume feature is very often mutually beneficial to choreographer, performer and costume designer since it allows for practical problem-solving early in the choreographic process rather than panic during later technical and dress rehearsals. You may even be inspired by having to experiment with what initially seems like an unwieldy costume. Check that the fabrics chosen will sustain reasonable wear and tear, frequent washing and drying or dry cleaning, and the rigours of touring with many performances per week.

In some kinds of production it is helpful to have items of costume to wear in rehearsal, though it may only be possible to have a rehearsal version of the required item. Check to see whether the item provided is identical in all important respects or just similar:

◆ If gloves are worn, check that any handling of people and props is possible and safe.

◆ If a cloak is used you may want to feel its weight and observe how the volume of material behaves.

◆ Hats may need the foundation of a wig or special hair arrangement. The method of fixing may be the result of experimentation in rehearsal.

◆ If a natural waistline has 'disappeared' under a costume, a safer partnering method may have to be devised.

## 4. Items for rehearsal— checklist

If sections of set, pieces of furniture, items of clothing are needed in rehearsal, try to provide advance warning and clear requests. A number of different designers or assistants, stage management or props department staff may need to be consulted (depending on the nature and scale of the production). Any requests, worries, criticisms about any of the items listed below should be noted down by the choreographer and a copy sent to the relevant department as well as the designer and/or assistant. Further discussion can then take place. Misdirected and unclear messages can lead to misunderstandings and bad feeling with consequent waste of time and money.

Check if you need to rehearse with any of the following:

+ Flooring: special surface, carpet, stretched canvas overlay, matting

+ Floor markings:to represent the extremities of the set or stage, wings, entrances, access steps, furniture, traps, flown props

+ Scenery: sections of set, flats, screens, masking, staircases, balustrades, balcony, window-frame, throne, rostrum, pavilion, fence, landscape, split-level staging, scaffolding, bridge, abstract construction, sculpture, moving panels

+ Furniture: chairs, tables, benches, beds

+ Props: lamps, candles, food, drink, crockery, luggage, books, flowers, juggling equipment, flags, stilts

+ Armoury: swords, daggers, knives, firearms, crossbows

+ Mechanical devices: wheelchairs, video monitors, film projectors, lifts, hydraulic equipment, bridges, moving panels

+ Vehicles: moved by remote, motor, animal or human power; cars, wagons, boats, carriages

+ Clothing:hats, veils, helmets, cloaks, shawls, scarves, jackets, coats, armour, underskirts, hoops, panniers, padding, prosthetics, shoes, boots

+ Accessories: gloves, handkerchiefs, walking sticks, crutches, fans

## 5. Floor surfaces

*On one occasion a designer showed me, for a floor surface, a sample of that bristly, green, doormat-quality artificial grass. The dancers were to be barefoot. After a short but firm exchange about high-speed turns and friction burns, the dancers were granted footwear.*

Kate Flatt, choreographer.

If you are using a special floor surface, technical and production staff will need to know that it can be laid, rolled or dismantled and stored quickly during an interval, for example, without damage to its 'reasonable' life. They also need to know or may advise on whether the special surface responds satisfactorily to brushing, washing or vacuuming.

What happens to the performers and the floor when the surface becomes wet with sweat or, if working in the open air, damp with dew or rain? Is it possible to perform on, does colour bleed, is there any shrinkage or change of texture?

If a complete body make-up is used, or liberal amounts of water, stage blood or other liquids, either on a performer or spread on the floor, or both, choreographer and designer should be aware that this may limit the amount of safe floor work and partnering possible by dancers.

Floor surfaces must be safe quite apart from their aesthetic suitability. Try to make sure that your designer is aware at the planning stage of the needs of the performers, whether they are working in pointe shoes, soft dance shoes with a variety of different soles, heeled boots, tap shoes, roller-skates, stilettos or bare feet.

Floor surfaces which are bristly, painted, textured or treated to appear worn, rough, outdoor, grassy, sandy or cobbled can produce quite severe bruises and grazes to the bare flesh of performers who are required to fall, roll, slide or be dragged on them. Any nails or tacks which are used to secure floor coverings to a basic floor or rostra must not stick out. The surface must be regularly inspected and any dislodged tacks must be removed and replaced.

The edges of floor coverings must have special attention, particularly at any joins in the material, at entrances and exists and on sloping surfaces and stairways.

## 6. Footwear

A designer who is not familiar with the needs of dancers must be prepared—or may need to be encouraged—to balance a dancer's practical needs with his or her ideas. Some designers may ignore, or may not be aware of, a dancer's need for comfortable footwear which is safe, flexible, and allows mobility and balance. Often there has to be some compromise. Both choreographer and designer may have to sacrifice an 'authentic look' in favour of the performers' safety and comfort.

Dancers and other performers will be very keen to test the designer's proposed footwear in the rehearsal studio and on the stage or performance surface, especially if this is raked. The use of costume footwear in rehearsal may be limited, depending on whether the production budget can stretch to duplicates. Remind the designer that performance footwear may need to be well 'worn in' in rehearsal to be fully comfortable in performance.

Footwear might need attention between rehearsals and first performance as well as during a season. Make sure the costume supervisor knows of any re-painting, cleaning, stretching or application of alternative soles which may be needed.

*See also:*

**Health and safety:**
Fireproofing (page 158)

**Lighting design** (page 136)

**Working as a choreographer:**
Rehearsals (Time to create the work) (page 33) Facilities (page 35)

**Working as a choreographer in opera and musical theatre:**
Dates and times (page 55)

**Copyright:**
Assignment and licence of copyright (page 153) Collaborations (page 154)

# Lighting design

In common with many other aspects of new choreographic work, some artistic and technical decisions about the lighting, and how to achieve it, should be made at an early stage, despite the fact that the plotting of the lighting design will take place shortly before the first performance of your work.

You may find it helpful to consult this chapter if you plan to light your work yourself. You may also find that a management or a lighting designer will ask you questions based on the matters listed, to ensure that lighting design is feasible within the production budget and possible within the production schedule. The subjects considered could apply to small or large-scale works, and provide the beginnings of a checklist when considering touring the production in the future.

1. What do you need?

2. The lighting session

3. Touring

## 1. What do you need?

✦ Will you be lighting the choreography yourself with the help of technicians?

✦ Will you be lighting the work yourself, and dancing in it too?

✦ Will you be using a lighting designer?

✦ If you have not worked with the lighting designer before, when will you meet, what do you know of his or her background and recent work, and will he or she be available to attend a sufficient number of your rehearsals?

✦ Is the venue for the first performance a fully-equipped space or theatre?

✦ Is the venue a completely empty space with power available?

✦ If you are working in an equipped space, will all equipment be available for your use, and will there be operators for the equipment, or any objections to your own technicians using it?

✦ Who will obtain detailed specifications about the venue?

✦ Will your choreography be the only work being performed, or will you or your lighting designer have to fit in with other works and share a lighting rig?

Your work might be an addition to two existing works in a triple bill, for example, or your choreography might be performed at a festival or charity gala, sharing an evening with other choreographers and companies. Find out where your work will be placed in the programme order. Make known in advance any special requests you may have in this respect.

The lighting will be affected by the environment and the equipment available, so find out or ask your lighting designer or technical assistant to obtain information. Look out for any limitations, especially with regard to the use of special lanterns or special effects.

Part of the skill of a lighting designer is the ability to assess what is feasible in a given situation in terms of time, location, budget and collaboration with the creative production team. A simple lighting design can be very effective and could be beneficial to the budget.

## 2. The lighting session

When studying the technical and staging rehearsal schedule issued by a commissioning company, or when organising your own company's schedule, check the time allocated for fitting up the set, rigging the lighting, focusing it, and plotting the cues with or without dancers present (according to your needs). It will help if the lighting designer, set and costume designer, and any other relevant people have attended rehearsals, and you all know what is to be achieved. It is an expensive luxury to keep technicians standing by while prolonged discussions take place about basic concepts.

The lighting session needs to involve the lighting designer, the choreographer, the person who will be calling the cues and 'running the show', and any technicians needed to operate equipment. You may also require dancers or a dancer to adopt the dancers' places on stage. If you are also dancing in the choreography, a substitute for yourself is helpful. If no dancers are available, ask a member of stage management, or other patient person, to 'walk' for you at the lighting session, possibly wearing or carrying one or more costumes if they are available. Lighting will considerably affect the colour and texture of costumes and vice versa.

The final timing of cues can best be fixed when music, sound sources and dancers are present, although timings taken at rehearsals should provide a very good starting point. Try to make time to re-run each cue and lighting state at the end of a plotting session.

Some choreographers have remarked that in their experience sufficient time has not been allocated in a lighting session for the lighting of curtain calls. If these are specially choreographed they will require lighting. It might be wise, where appropriate, to check the speed of any front curtains or 'house tabs' prior to the lighting session. If their clearing and closing speed is too slow for the pace of the previous choreography, or inappropriate for the curtain call, you may wish to use a blackout instead.

Neither choreographer nor lighting designer, dancers nor technical staff, should have to work all day and night if it can be avoided. You and your colleagues will work less efficiently and safely if you are tired, so avoid overnight lighting sessions if at all possible.

It is advisable, if you have limited technical assistance, to check that dancers can get safely on and off stage without tripping, or hitting or toppling lighting stands in the wings or at the edge of the performance area. Also check that performers can see their way safely in semi-darkness from dressing rooms to stage. Pay particular attention to access steps and stairways. At the first stage rehearsal, if you observe that there are problems with lights shining in such a way as to cause the dancers problems

with their balance and focus, you may have to make adjustments.

## 3. Touring

If you have designed the lighting for your own work, keep the plot and a photocopy (or back-up disc if plotted on computer) safely for future reference in the event of a revival in the same venue or for possible adaptation on tour.

The wider subject of touring demands more extensive consideration than suggested by the following advice, but, in brief:

If you are planning a tour to a variety of theatres or spaces, you and the venues need to establish well in advance a clear understanding of your requirements. Ask the venue for details of sight-lines, staging and lighting resources, and available technical staff. If some or all of the venues are under-equipped, consider the possibility of hiring and touring your own lighting rig and control desk, so that, with careful planning and following detailed enquiries, you are able to re-create the same situation in each venue. You may be able to augment your rig with the theatre or venue's own equipment. If you are equipped with your own basic set-up, and have cue-states stored in the lighting desk, plotting time can be kept short, especially if you have the assistance of an experienced technician.

*See also:*

**Set and costume design** (page 130)

**Health and safety** (page 156)

**Working as a choreographer:**
Rehearsals (Time to create the work) (page 33)
The choreography (Full evening works and mixed programmes) (page 32)
Pre- and post-production meetings (page 38)

# Videotapes

People tend to think of videotapes as robust and permanent commodities. They are neither. This chapter provides some guidelines on their use, preservation and storage.

1. Making

2. Labelling

3. Copying

4. Storing

5. Travelling by air

6. Format

## 1. Making

Before a video recording of your choreography is made, check that all parties have consented to the recording: performers, composers, musicians, set and costume designers, lighting designer, technicians, the venue, and anyone else involved. Do not assume that permission has been granted. Secure consent in writing for future reference.

If you are making your own video recording, use equipment that is clean and serviced on a regular basis. It is essential that all leads, power cables, batteries and tapes are checked the day before recording, and again on the day of recording. You could make a preliminary recording and familiarise yourself with the controls, then play it back. Use a tripod. Alternatively, ask someone who is familiar with video technique in studio or performance conditions to make the recording for you. Use mains power rather than batteries if you can. If not, ensure that all batteries, including spares, are fully charged (this takes some time).

Do not record over old works for your master tape. This tends to degrade the quality of the finished recording. Try to use separate tapes for each choreographic work unless you are certain that a number of short works can be included on one tape.

There is a considerable difference in quality between tape brands so buy the best quality you can afford. If you want to ensure that your equipment and your recording have the best chance of survival, buy professional tapes.

Immediately the recording has finished, remove the security tab to prevent accidental erasure. Label and date the tape, and make a note of the duration of the recording.

## 2. Labelling

As soon as possible after the recording, label and date the cassette sleeve and box. Try to include as much information as possible for future reference by yourself or others in your absence: fix a typed list to the box containing the name of the choreographer, the date and location of the recording, whether it was a rehearsal or a performance, the name of the composer and musicians or sound source, the title of the music or sound score, the names of lighting, set and costume designers and the name of the company or the performers. A programme is a useful source of additional information, but if this is stored with the videotape, check that the people who performed were, in fact, those listed in it.

Subject to your agreement, video recordings of your work may be used by a notator in conjunction with a movement score for educational or revival purposes. Video recordings may be used by others for a variety of purposes without any additional record of the choreography. Instead of being seen as an independent visual record of one rehearsal or performance of the work, the video will tend to be treated by future casts, research students and historians as the definitive record or 'authorised version'. It is therefore important to share with your notator, assistant, artistic director, archivist or rehearsal director your thoughts on the video's accuracy and merits. Attach these comments to the video, or record a commentary onto the video itself. Lodge a copy of your comments with any or all of the aforementioned staff.

Inexpensive plastic cassette boxes will keep your tape and any notes safe and secure.

## 3. Copying

A small kit of cables (usually marketed as a <u>universal scart/camcorder kit</u>) will ensure that you have the necessary connections to make video copies.

If the recording is yours, make a back-up copy as soon as possible. Do not assume that the tape will last indefinitely. Store the original and only use a copy for viewing purposes. Label and date the copy in the same manner as the original.

Remember that it is illegal to make copies of commercial recordings. You are also depriving fellow artists of royalty payments. Bear in mind that choreography that is 'fixed' by video recording is protected under copyright law. You should be aware of agreements and permissions which may be attached to those video recordings, and any limitations which may apply, whether the recordings were made by you, borrowed, or bought commercially. You should not abuse those agreements unless you are prepared to suffer the consequences of legal action.

If you are showing a commercial video in public, you will need a licence from Video Performance Limited.

*See also:*
**Useful addresses:**
Phonographic Performance Limited (booklet)

## 4. Storing

Whether you store videotapes in a company office or archive for future viewing, or whether you store them at home as part of your 'portfolio' for promotional purposes, the storage conditions are very important to observe.

If you do not have the luxury of proper light, heat and temperature-controlled conditions, try to avoid storing tapes on open shelves in direct sunlight. Avoid direct heat from appliances. Avoid exposure to moisture and humid conditions. A safe temperature range is 10-18°C. Keep tapes inside their cases and in some kind of cabinet or container to avoid dust and dirt. Keep tapes away from strong magnetic fields. Transformers and loudspeakers are magnets.

Try to ensure that the storage place you have chosen for the videos is fire-resistant and not directly underneath a bath or shower room or water tank. Store videotapes vertically (like a book), as storage on their sides will lead to distortion. For added security do not store the master tape and copy in the same location.

Videotapes which form part of a company archive are best kept somewhere you can lock. It is advisable to supervise access and usage of the collection.

View the tapes yearly, or at least once in every three years, and make a further back-up copy at the first sign of deterioration of quality.

## 5. Travelling by air

When travelling by air, take your videotape with you as cabin baggage. At baggage or security checkpoints, ask the airport personnel to check the tape manually and not to put it through the X-ray machine as it is the strong magnetic fields produced by this that can damage your tape.

Be aware that airport personnel in any country may want to view any videotapes you are carrying. This may be part of their normal procedure to counter the importation of pornographic, anti-government or anti-religious material. The choreographic content of your tape may not be considered indecent or in any way offensive in the UK, but a passionate or violent duet could be regarded as defamatory in other countries with different moral traditions and religious beliefs. The penalties for carrying such material could be severe and any delay caused could be very inconvenient.

## 6. Format

You may wish to play tapes back for pleasure, to show a prospective management, to refresh your memory in advance of a revival of your work, or to observe work made from a tape made by someone else—possibly from another country. Video pictures are recorded in several different formats—systems and standards—in different parts of the world, and it is important to be aware of the differences.

The standard is the technical definition of how the information which makes up a picture is transmitted and reproduced. This is 'country-specific'. For example, North America and Japan use NTSC standard. Most of Europe uses the PAL standard, but France, the countries of the former USSR and most of Eastern Europe use the SECAM standard.

The system is the technical definition of how the information which makes up the picture is recorded or stored on a physical medium. This is 'manufacturer-specific'. For example, VHS is a widely-used and easily available system. Video 8 is a common system for small camcorders.

You will not be able to play one system's tapes in another system's video machine. You may well damage the tape if you try to do this. Unless you have access to some costly equipment, you cannot interchange standards. With detailed information sent in advance you may be able to hire the correct playback equipment or have the tape professionally transferred to your own standard or system.

If you plan to send one of your tapes to be viewed by someone else, provide in advance the details which will enable that person to view it or have it transferred to the relevant standard or system. Make a note of any tape you send away, with the date it was posted, and make sure that your tape is returned to you if that is part of the arrangement.

It is unwise to part with your only video recording of one particular work.

*See also:*
**Copyright** (page 151)

**Assistants, notators and staff producers: NOTATORS** (page 114)

PART 5

# PART 5

Insurance

Copyright

Health and safety

Child performance
regulations

# Insurance

The information provided in this chapter is an outline for guidance only. You are strongly advised to consult a professional insurance broker regarding your needs before entering into any agreement.

The chapter aims to help the process of considering and obtaining different types of insurance, and it may serve as a point of reference for choreographers and their assistants when seeking headings from which to select the insurance which may be necessary for their next project or commission.

1. Insurance broker

2. The choreographer as employer

3. The choreographer as freelance artist

## 1. Insurance broker

An insurance broker considers a client's requirements and decides how best to serve them by obtaining the best terms from among those offered by different insurance companies. It is important to consult a registered insurance broker, and that he or she has knowledge of the entertainment industry. Well-founded recommendations from colleagues could be a starting point in the search for a suitable broker. You can also get a list of brokers from the British Insurance and Investment Brokers Association (BIIBA), or consult Equity or Dance UK.

*See also:*
**Useful addresses** (booklet)

## 2. The choreographer as employer

If you are the employer-leader of a company or small group, hiring dancers or other performers for your project, season of performances or tour, you need to consider the types of insurance you must have by law and those which you would be well-advised to have. Discuss the types of insurance with your broker and whether they should be short-term policies or annual insurances. A broker may be able to arrange a package policy which covers some or all of the following headings:

### Insurance you are required to have by law:

*Employer's Liability*
This covers claims made against you by employees (your dancers and staff) for injury at work caused by your negligence. You are required to display the relevant certificate at your place of work and at each venue on tour.

*Motor*
This covers insurance for any van, car or motorbike, hired or owned and used by you or your employees. Check that the insurance is the right type and covers the appropriate usage. Make sure that if your employee is using his or her own vehicle for your business, the class of use under his or her policy is adequate. Also make sure you have a Motor Contingency Extension under your Public Liability policy.

It is becoming increasingly difficult and expensive to insure mini-buses. This expense should be borne in mind when compiling a budget for your project. You may find it beneficial to try and hire the mini-bus from a company which can also provide insurance for the vehicle. Check that the insurance company which issues the policy is aware of your occupation.

### Insurance you may wish to consider:

*All Risks*
A standard theatrical policy will cover the insurance of loss or damage to scenery, props, costumes, sound, lighting and video equipment in respect of property owned or hired by you, or for which you are responsible, for a particular production on site and on tour in the UK. Ask the broker for details of all policy exclusions such as theft from unattended vehicles without an adequate alarm system. Also check the policy 'excess' — the sum deducted from an insurer's repayment to you in the event of a claim made for loss or damage etc.

*Public Liability*
Public liability is also known as Third Party Insurance, and often required as a condition of contract. It covers your

146

liability for damage to public property and your liability for injury to the public. Make sure the limit of indemnity is adequate.

### Money

Cover could include the theft or loss of cash (petty cash or money in transit to or from the bank), and cover, for example, for an employee who is mugged while carrying company money.

*Note that if you are arranging a theatrical package insurance, you must make sure that all the insurance is effective from the date of first rehearsal and not from the date of first performance.*

### Cancellation/Abandonment

Sometimes it might be necessary to take out insurance against the following:

✦ the abandonment of an outdoor event due to bad weather

✦ the potential non-appearance of a 'star' performer due to sickness or death

✦ the cancellation of an event, and consequent financial loss, due to fire, serious vandalism of property, epidemic, major power failure, etc.

This is a complicated type of insurance. The wording of the policy is very important and tailored to individual needs.

### Office

If your group's headquarters are in rented office space you should consider an office package which provides cover for office equipment, money, employer's liability and public liability, etc.

If your group's headquarters are at home, you should ask your household insurers if they are prepared to include your group's office contents as an extension to your household policy. If you fail to tell your insurers that your home includes office equipment and resources belonging to your group, you could invalidate your home building and contents insurance **but** it is unlikely that household insurers will also give you Public/Employer's Liability.

### Group Travel

A group travel insurance policy should include the standard risks found in a holiday insurance **but** a holiday travel package will probably not be adequate as there will be exclusions such as 'manual work'.

Cover should include the following types of insurance:

✦ Personal Baggage

✦ Personal Money

✦ Medical and Other Expenses

✦ Emergency Assistance Service

✦ Replacement Expenses (replacing an artist)

✦ Cancellation or Curtailment Charges

✦ Personal Accident

✦ Personal Liability

✦ Departure Delay

Bear in mind that if you are working under an Equity contract there are minimum levels of cover written into the Standard Overseas Agreement.

### Group Personal Accident

This is an insurance against accidents for each individual—a group-rate policy for people with similar risk occupations. Dance UK operates a Group Personal Accident Scheme. Details available from Dance UK's office.

*See also:*
**Dance UK** (page iv)

## 2. The choreographer as freelance artist

When working anywhere in the UK or abroad it is important to have insurance which is sufficiently comprehensive and appropriate to your usual occupation, adequate for all your destinations and of adequate duration.

When working for a commissioning company or an educational establishment, it is likely that the company's or educational body's general insurance might automatically provide some cover in the event of a claim made against you or by you while working for that company in or on its property. You are advised to check with the company, college, local authority, etc. what your insurance position is before starting work. Be aware that if an injury to a performer results from an instruction given by you while you are conducting an audition or while you are choreographing, there is a potential liability against you. Although you may be protected by the insurance of the commissioning organisation, you may not be protected from a counter-claim from that insurance company. It is advisable to satisfy yourself at the beginning of a period of employment that you are protected by insurance, your or your employer's, for any claim made against you or your choreography as the cause of an injury or accident in rehearsal or performance.

**Insurance you may wish to consider:**

*Household*
This insurance covers general household contents. Check with your insurance broker which of the following types of insurance may need to be added. (The following are extensions to the basic package and cannot be insured in isolation). You should examine all the small print, exclusion clauses, and excess limits which may apply:

*Personal Possessions/All Risks*
This insurance (which is an extension of a household contents policy) will include clothing, luggage, and certain categories of valuables which may include jewellery, watches, cameras, musical instruments, personal computers, compact disc players, etc. and limited personal money. If the items are being used for your business they cannot normally be insured under your household insurance and will require a separate insurance policy. Remember to extend the geographical areas covered by your policy if planning to work abroad.

*Travel*
If you are going abroad on business this policy should include the standard risks found in a holiday insurance **but** a holiday travel package will probably not be adequate as there will be exclusions such as 'manual work'. A business travel policy will suffice but make sure that insurers are aware of your occupation and that you do not breach any integral exclusions.

Cover should include the following types of insurance:

+ **Personal Money** (this insurance will include cash, travellers' cheques, etc.)

+ **Personal Baggage** (check the insurance limits for valuables and any single article)

+ **Personal Accident** (this will cover death, loss of limbs etc. for a lump sum)

## Medical and Other Expenses

Some countries have no national health service and the cost of private medical treatment can be very high. Even in the countries of the European Community with which the UK has mutual health care arrangements, these arrangements may not cover all the expenses you can incur. Form E111 should be obtained from the Post Office for travel to countries within the EC plus Austria, Finland, Iceland, Norway and Sweden. This form gives you access to free or reduced-cost emergency treatment on the same terms as nationals. Private treatment is not covered, nor is repatriation (bringing a person back to the UK in the event of illness or death) which can be very expensive. It is sensible to keep a photocopy of your E111 form, as you may need a copy for reference if you have to part with the original form.

## Emergency Assistance Service

This type of insurance includes a 24 hour, multi-lingual helpline and emergency assistance service.

## Cancellation or Curtailment Charges

Charges could arise from, for example, the necessary cancellation or curtailment of your journey as a result of your, or a close relative's illness, or from your necessary presence for jury service or as a witness in a court of law.

## Departure Delay

You may wish to be compensated for the failure of public transport scheduled services, and subsequent delay or abandonment of the journey.

## Personal Liability

This insurance covers your liability for damage to another person's property, or your accidental injury to another person.

## Other types of insurance you may wish to consider:

## Personal Accident/Sickness/ Permanent Health

It is advisable to take out a Personal Accident and Sickness Policy to cover yourself. A Permanent Health Insurance Policy is also an option. The main difference between these types is that a Personal Accident and Sickness Policy caters for short-term disability in which you receive a weekly amount for up to 104 weeks, and also provides in respect of Personal Accident a lump sum in the event of death, loss of limbs and permanent total disablement. The Permanent Health Insurance Policy is designed to pay a monthly sum from the end of the 'waiting' period (normally four to 13 weeks) until your normal retirement date. Dance is usually classed a 'hazardous' occupation as far as this type of insurance is concerned. You or your broker should check that the wording is particular with reference to permanent total disablement from your 'usual' occupation, not just 'any' occupation.

149

## Loss of Earnings

The assumption that it is impossible to obtain insurance to cover loss of earnings is incorrect, although it may be difficult to find terms at an economic rate. An experienced broker who understands your specific requirements and is aware of the risks involved may be able to obtain an acceptable insurance solution for an individual or group.

## Special Effects

If you are working with special equipment or effects you should consult the company for whom you are working and/ or take qualified advice on the need for any additional insurance which may be necessary. The involvement of fire, flying, fights, trap-doors, animal handling, hydraulics, jumping from heights, etc. may require special insurance/inspection.

## Motor

If you plan to drive outside the UK consult your broker or one of the principal motoring organisations to make sure you are fully covered.

## Legal Protection

Legal Protection policies offer the use of a 24 hour legal helpline and protection against legal bills if you need to employ a professional to pursue claims for you. This is usually available as an extension to a household insurance policy.

*See also:*

**Health and safety** (page 156)

**Working abroad** (page 103)

**Working as a choreographer for a specific site or occasion:organisation** (page 96)

# Copyright

It is essential to establish the ownership of the copyright of the choreographic work you are being paid to create, and to know what rights you have over your works. It is also important to respect the copyright in other people's work that you may be using—music, photographs, graphic design, set and costume design, sound recordings. If in any doubt, consult your agent or a qualified professional adviser. This chapter may help you to understand how copyright works.

1. What is copyright?

2. Legislation

3. What works can have copyright protection?

4. Who owns copyright?

5. What action is needed to give copyright protection?

6. Periods of copyright protection and public domain

7. Permitted acts

8. Assignment and licence of copyright

9. International arrangements

10. Remedies for infringement of copyright

11. Moral rights

12. Collaborations

13. Further use

14. Using other people's copyright works

## 1. What is Copyright?

Copyright protects your work from being copied, issued in copies to the public, performed in public or broadcast without your permission, including in an adapted form.

## 2. Legislation

The latest legislation, the 1988 Copyright, Designs and Patents Act, applies to people living in the UK and to copying done here from 1 August 1989 onwards.

## 3. What works can have copyright protection?

The work must be 'original'—not be copied from somewhere else. Copyright legislation categorises works: dance comes under 'dramatic works', music under 'musical works'. Literary works are also covered, as are film, broadcast, sound recordings and typographical arrangements of published editions.

Theatrical productions or dance collaborations are not recognised as copyright works in their own right, but contain many copyright works. Sound recordings have separate copyright from the music or other material that is recorded. Adaptations and arrangements can have copyright protection. However, names and titles are not covered by copyright.

## 4. Who owns copyright?

For literary, dramatic, musical and artistic works, the artist—for example, choreographer, composer, designer or photographer—will be the first owner of copyright **if they are freelance**, unless a written contract states otherwise.

Where a **freelance artist is commissioned to produce a work**, the artist will be the first owner of copyright, unless a written contract states otherwise.

Where the artist is **employed**, the company will be the first owner of copyright unless a written contract states otherwise.

Where the artist is a **student**, the college will be the first owner of copyright and this is usually stated in the college's rules.

The first owner of copyright in sound recordings is whoever makes the arrangements necessary to produce the recording. This is usually the record company or, in some circumstances, a freelance sound engineer.

It is professional good practice to have clarification of copyright issues in a written contract.

## 5. What action is needed to give copyright protection?

Dance and music works have to be 'fixed' by recording, by video or notation to have copyright protection. Prior to 1 August 1989, dance had to be notated—video did not count as 'fixing' it, though now it does. Other than 'fixing', no action is needed to confer copyright protection—once the work is created and fixed it enjoys copyright.

A choreographer may wish to impose or negotiate limitations on the usage of movement notation scores and videos, on who holds copies and who uses them for rehearsal or re-staging purposes. These agreements should be in writing and distributed to all relevant parties.

It is worth considering practices that prove a piece of work was in your possession at a given time. The most common of these is to send a tape or written record of your work to yourself by recorded delivery, leave it unopened until you need it as evidence, and then open it in front of witnesses.

## 6. Periods of copyright protection and public domain

If a work is not protected by copyright legislation, it is said to be 'in the public domain'. In the UK dance, music, designs, photographs, for instance, are protected for the author's life plus 70 years from the end of the year of the author's death. This recent change of legislation (previously 50 years) means that some works which were out of copyright, under the 50 year rule, will go back into copyright, as the law will be applied retrospectively. For joint authorship the term is the longest surviving author's life plus 70 years. Films and sound recordings are protected for 70 years from when they are made or released.

*See also:*
**Music:**
The use of live and recorded music in public (page 121)

## 7. Permitted acts

Some specific uses of copyright works are permitted without the owner's permission. These include:

✦ research and private study—you may make a single photocopy of a document or excerpt if it is to be used for your own preparation work or writing, for instance.

✦ review and criticism—you may make multiple copies of a document or excerpt (for inclusion, for example, in programme notes) but must give an acknowledgement of work and author.

✦ reporting of current events.

✦ special provisions for educational establishments, libraries and archives.

Performances given for the purposes of instruction, in an educational establishment, with an audience of pupils or students only (and accompanying teachers), do not count as public performances for copyright purposes.

There is an exemption from licensing for the use of sound recordings (not the music in them) for organisations that are charities and where the income from admissions is applied only to the organisation.

## 8. Assignment and licence of copyright

Copyright, as with other forms of property, can be bought, sold, 'let' or given away. The two main ways of dealing with copyright are 'assigning', which is equivalent to selling, and 'licensing' which is equivalent to letting.

Assigning copyright means that it then belongs to the new owner. Assignments must be in writing and signed by the assignor.

Licensing copyright gives others permission to make specific use of it. Exclusive licences mean that no other person can be given the same rights. Exclusive licences must be in writing and signed by the licensor. A company may negotiate exclusive rights to perform one (or more) of your works for a specified number of performances or years and may negotiate a first option to renew the rights to perform that work for a further specified period. This means that if another company shows interest in that choreography you are not at liberty to respond for the duration of the exclusive period. Upon expiry of the exclusive rights you could re-negotiate with the first company and negotiate with another company (perhaps abroad) to present the same choreography simultaneously.

Remember that some companies will expect the copyright in the choreography to be assigned to them. The price for such an assignment is usually high and often includes payment to the choreographer each time the work is used. Seek professional advice.

Check the wording of a commissioning company's ownership of the copyright of your choreography in the contract with specific reference to the way that it is recorded or preserved. You may want to limit the number of media, distribution networks and period of time over which it can be reproduced.

Performers are protected against their performances being recorded in any medium without their permission. This protection lasts for 50 years from the performance.

## 9. International arrangements

Copyright conventions cover most of the world giving copyright protection almost everywhere. Copyright protection works on the terms of the domestic legislation of the country within which it is claimed. In some countries (but not in the UK) you are required to use the copyright symbol and/or by-line to register your work:

© *Artist's (or copyright owner's) name, date. All rights reserved.*

## 10. Remedies for infringement of copyright

It is possible to get a court injunction to prevent infringement (unauthorised use) of copyright. You can claim damages, and an account of profits gained by the infringer. While names and titles are not protected by copyright, you can prevent somebody seeking to imitate your product or company, under common law, by an action for 'passing off'. In this case, you would need to contact a solicitor or legal adviser.

## 11. Moral rights

Artists have the right to be identified as the authors of their work but must specifically assert this by using appropriate wording:

*The right of [name] to be identified as Author of this work has been asserted by [name] in accordance with the Copyright, Designs and Patents Act 1988.*

For a dance work on video, this should appear on the title sequence and on labels.

Artists have the right not to have their work added to, deleted from, altered, or adapted in such a way that amounts to distortion or mutilation of the work, or which is prejudicial to the honour or reputation of the maker. Artists may be asked to waive these rights, but they should think carefully before agreeing to do so, and there should be some financial benefit to them if they do agree to a waiver.

## 12. Collaborations

In the case of a collaborative work, it is appropriate to make the copyright ownership reflect the individuals' contribution to the creative process. It is good practice to have a written agreement that clearly states the proportions owned by each collaborator. If they wish to do so, the collaborators/copyright owners can insist that elements of the collaboration (for instance, the music and dance) can only be used together in the future.

## 13. Further use

An agreement between an artist and the company, or between artists within a collaboration, should state clearly what system will apply for further use of the work, covering permission for the use, credits, and royalties. If one person is appointed to give permissions for further use, then discussion and agreement is needed on what uses are acceptable.

## 14. Using other people's copyright works

It is important to respect the copyright works of others and, if you are making use of them or incorporating them into your own work, only do so with permission.

*See also:*
**Contract** (page 3)

**Assistants, notators and staff producers:**
**NOTATORS:** Ownership, security and use (page 116)

**Videotapes** (page 139)

# Health and safety

This chapter outlines steps you should take at the beginning of every new job or project to ensure that your working environment is as safe as possible. It is especially important to pay attention to these procedures if you are a choreographer leading a company without a substantial administrative and technical management and/or in a variety of rehearsal and performance spaces where support staff may not be readily available in the case of an accident. This advice is, however, relevant to anyone, whether they are working in a theatre, church hall, tent or warehouse.

If you are touring abroad you will need to comply with the health and safety regulations of each country you visit.

1. First steps

2. First aid

3. AIDS/HIV prevention

4. Fire precautions

5. Fireproofing

6. During rehearsals

7. Special effects or equipment

8. Performance and backstage areas

When working under contract for a company or institution, or directing your own group, it is your responsibility to take 'reasonable precautions' against injury during the rehearsal period.

Health and safety laws use vague terms such as 'reasonable', 'adequate' and 'sufficient'. Although the company or institution with whom the choreographer is working is responsible for the overall safety procedures of any production, the choreographer must ensure that he or she cannot be proved negligent if an accident occurs during the rehearsal process. If an accident does occur, and it is proved that the choreographer concerned has **not** taken reasonable precautions against such an event, then she or he will have to deal with any consequences, and even face court proceedings (as the company is unlikely to pay any fines that are imposed). **It is imperative, therefore, to be able to prove that you have taken steps to protect the people working with you before any such accident occurs. Although health and safety issues are the mutual responsibility of both choreographer and management, if you are proved negligent when management can prove it has taken 'reasonable' steps, it will be you who are penalised.**

## 1. First steps

If in doubt about a company's or other institution's health and safety regulations, contact your agent or Equity for advice. You may be asked to complete a declaration as part of your contract, stating that you are properly qualified and insured to do the job you have been employed to do (this may imply a management or supervisory role over those working for you, even if you have been employed purely as a choreographer).

Find out who is responsible for health and safety before you start the rehearsal process. A well-organised company will automatically provide you with a health and safety document and show you its health and safety procedures on arrival. If it does not, you should ask the health and safety officer or personnel manager the following questions :

## 2. First aid

✦ Where are the first aid boxes kept? Are they properly equipped for the needs of dancers and who is responsible for their supplies?

✦ If the first aid box is kept locked, who has the key? Where is the key kept after 'normal' office hours?

✦ Who are the qualified **first-aiders** in the company or group? Are there first-aiders among dancing and management personnel?

✦ Is there a telephone in or near the rehearsal area?

✦ Where is the **accident report book** kept, and who is responsible for its upkeep? In the case of any accident, enter the details into the accident report book as precisely as possible — the name of the patient; date, time and circumstances of the accident; details of injury suffered and treatment given; the names of any witnesses. This record will be essential in any court case that occurs as a result of the injury, and a court or tribunal may look upon its absence as evidence of your negligence.

Dance UK publishes an Information Sheet, *Dancer's First Aid Box* , providing advice in the event of minor injury or ill-ness, plus a checklist for the contents of a first aid box (rather than a first aid store). A first aid box would be a very important part of your equipment if you were leading a small group in relatively unsophisticated rehearsal studios.

*See also:*
**Dance UK resources** (page v)

## 3. AIDS/HIV prevention

As in any workplace, it is wise to avoid blood to blood contact in the event of injury in order to prevent the possible spread of HIV (Human Immuno-Deficiency Virus). Make sure that the first aid box of any company is equipped with dis-posable plastic gloves which should be used routinely whenever there is the chance of direct blood contact. Cover scrapes and cuts with clean, dry band-ages, and try to avoid the sharing of pointe shoes — or any shoes in which blood may be present.

Contact the company's personnel manager if you want to know its HIV/AIDS (Acquired Immune Deficiency Syndrome) policy, or if you need information about support services or telephone helplines.

*See also:*
**Useful addresses:**
Dance Cares (booklet)
Aids helpline (booklet)

## 4. Fire precautions

✦ What are the fire precautions and procedures?

✦ Are smoking areas clearly marked?

✦ Is there a fire alarm which can be heard throughout the building?

✦ Where are the nearest fire extin-guishers, buckets and blankets?

✦ Where are the nearest fire exits?

Fire doors should **never** be locked when people are in the building.

If you are directing your own group in rented rehearsal studios, ask your dancers, any other performers and staff to attend a short talk on the first day of rehearsals. If there is a security officer or caretaker on the premises, ask him to brief you all. If not, inform those present yourself. Point out the fire exits, refresh-ment area, smoking area (if any), first aid box, washing facilities and drinking water points (if any). Explain and run through the fire drill. Make a note of the date on which you held this health and safety talk and list those present. Again, in the event of an investigation, a written record of your efforts to follow the correct procedures will be valuable evidence of your competence and sense of responsib-ility.

## 5. Fireproofing

All choreographers, particularly those who are also the director/administrators of small groups and therefore carry multiple responsibilities, should be aware that the designer of the set and/or costumes and/or special effects must produce designs which, when complete, conform to the local authority fire regulations. These regulations can be supplied to you by each venue at which your production will appear. There may be slight differences between each authority's regulations, and regulations may differ between various types of venue — for example, open stage, studio theatre, proscenium arch with a safety curtain (or 'fire iron'). Check with each venue, declaring everything applicable, including items such as flash-boxes and other effects.

As a precaution against future problems, you should warn designers that anything they provide must comply with fire regulations. This warning could be particularly important for someone who is not a qualified theatre designer but who has kindly offered to make a piece of scenery, staging or furniture for you at a cost which suits your budget.

All materials for set, staging, curtains, gauzes, borders, masking and so on and some props and furniture must conform to British Standard flame tests. They must be either constructed of inherently flame-retardant material or, in the case of wood, be of a grade and thickness to satisfy the fire regulations or be chemically treated to be sufficiently flame-retardant.

Certain materials which are flammable (such as some plastics) which cannot be treated and therefore would not be approved should be avoided. Any pyrotechnic, smoke machine, confetti canon, fog machine or similar special effect will also require approval by the fire officer.

Ask the venue if the fire officer (usually the local authority environmental health officer) can be contacted in advance. Can you send samples of materials or book a time for his visit?

A local authority fire officer can visit a theatre or other performance venue unannounced to carry out a spot check and test any of your scenery and materials. His or her technique is simple and immediate—setting light or attempting to set light to any solid structure or soft fabric and watching the result to see if the material self-

extinguishes within a given time. If the officer is unhappy with the findings, he or she will forbid the use of the offending structure or material, which could prevent performance.

Costumes do not have to be made with flame-retardant materials **unless** they are fixed to the set, are extraordinarily large or could come into contact with a naked flame on stage or in the wings or access areas.

## 6. During rehearsals

Health and safety for dancers involves a far wider set of issues than a simple concern for the prevention of accidents. It is important to treat your dancers and yourself with care throughout the rehearsal period. Make sure that the day is divided into manageable rehearsal periods with adequate breaks for resting and eating. If you have to go outside the building to get lunch, make sure that enough time is allowed for digestion and energy recovery before the next session. Find out if any of your dancers are also performing in a different production in the evenings. Be aware that their energy and concentration levels may be affected by early morning classes and rehearsals over a busy period.

If you are choreographing in an innovative way which is new to the dancers, be aware that this may cause strain if it is repetitive, violent or draws for too long on their emotional resources. If you are working with alternative casts, they may have different physiques from those of the first cast and you may need to vary your choreography slightly to suit different skills.

## 7. Special effects and equipment

If you are working with special equipment it is important to make sure that both the company for whom you are working and your dancers are insured, fit and qualified to do these things. Consider the following:

+ Electrical equipment
+ Using torches or candles
+ Fights with armoury
+ Firearms
+ Using fire
+ Using water
+ Handling animals
+ Flying
+ Hydraulics
+ Smoke, fog, dry ice, cracked oil
+ Trap doors, concealed entrances
+ Stilts
+ Lifting and carrying people, furniture, sections of set

The company will need a special licence to enable it to use firearms, naked flames and animals in rehearsal and performance.

Will it be necessary to invite a qualified instructor to provide tuition on the use and safety of special equipment? A safety officer may need to be present at all rehearsals and performances.

There is very real concern about the number of back injuries caused by inappropriate 'manual handling' (lifting). As a dancer and choreographer it should be safe to assume that you have been trained to lift in the correct manner and are alert to hazards. If, during the course of a rehearsal, it becomes clear that a lift or some other movement is potentially dangerous, you should stop it or make it safe.

*See also:*
**Insurance** (page 145)

**Working as a choreographer:**
Casting (Animals and birds) (page 41)

## 8. Performance and backstage areas

You may have a company manager or technical staff to assess and maintain backstage conditions. If not it is wise to check these areas yourself, particularly when you are on a tour that takes you to a different venue every few days:

+ Is the performance area clean, adequately lit for rehearsal purposes, heated and ventilated?

+ Are all the sets, props and equipment securely fixed and safe?

+ Are any backstage or belowstage passageways clearly lit?

+ Is there an emergency lighting system in the event of a power failure?

+ Are passageways clear of obstacles?

+ Are staircases properly treaded?

+ Are the dressing rooms clean and tidy, with adequate lighting, heating, ventilation, furniture and mirrors?

+ Are the dressing rooms cleaned on a regular basis?

+ Are there enough dressing rooms to avoid overcrowding?

+ Is there hot and cold water, showers, and baths if necessary?

+ Is there any drinking water?

+ Is there somewhere secure to keep valuables?

Make sure that any props, scenery, lighting equipment and cables do not impinge on the performers' safety. Check that both the performance and rehearsal area floor are safe and adequate for dance. If there is a section of carpet or flooring laid over the basic floor surface, make sure that it is securely fixed and that the edges will not cause the performers to trip.

*See also:*
**Working as a choreographer:**
Rehearsals (Facilities) (page 35)

**Insurance** (page 145)

**Set and costume design:**
Floor surfaces (page 134)

# Child performance regulations

In most cases, certainly when working for large companies, the responsibility for the welfare of children who take part in public performances is not primarily that of the choreographer. However, for your own information and understanding, it is always worth checking with your Local Authority Education Department (LAED) on the special regulations which will apply.

If the law is broken it is the named person to whom the licence has been granted who would be prosecuted and not any other representatives of the theatre or dance company itself.

1. Summary of regulations

2. Examples of exceptions

3. General notes

4. Working abroad

If the company you are working for has a children's manager, try to make time for you (and your assistant) to discuss the limitations on the children's working hours. Ask for a summary of the restrictions in order to avoid any mistakes. The children's availability will directly affect your choreographic planning, rehearsal schedules and fittings amongst other things. A children's manager will not take kindly to a late evening telephone call which announces a change in the following day's rehearsal schedule for the children. Although this is sometimes unavoidable, the children's manager is faced with a host of calls to parents at night, to the schools in the morning, and to chaperones and transport drivers. The LAED should also be notified of timetable alterations.

When contacting the LAED, ask for the Educational Welfare Service (which is usually the department in which your enquiry will be directed to the relevant officer).

## 1. Summary of regulations

This is a summary of the extensive regulations and procedures attached to the Children and Young Persons Act 1963 section 37 – The Children (performances) Regulations 1968 – and is applicable to 5-16 year-olds. These regulations also apply to children who attend theatre schools:

Each child or young person needs an individual licence which will be issued (if there is agreement) by the child's LAED. This is based on the child's home address and not on the location of the school. Applications must be made at least 21 days before any period of rehearsal or performance. When the LAED receives the application for a licence, it must be sure that in agreeing to issue one, the child's

education will not suffer. The LAED will contact the child's head teacher to check on his or her views before agreeing to issue the licence.

The licence must be completed by a parent or guardian and by the applicant (the company 'employing' the children). The school or college must give its consent. A copy of the child's birth certificate and a medical certificate are required, as well as two recent, identical photographs.

The regulations vary according to age group but will concern (in short):

✦ a minimum number of hours of education required per day on school days

✦ a maximum number of hours of attendance at rehearsal and performance per day

✦ an earliest and latest permitted time at the place of rehearsal and performance

✦ prescribed intervals for meals and rest

## 2. Examples of exceptions

There are several circumstances when a licence under the performance regulations (1968) is not required. For example:

✦ If the child will not be required to be absent from school for rehearsal or performance.

✦ If the child participates in a charity performance at which the public pays no charge and if the rehearsal is on a Saturday with the performance on a Sunday (up to a maximum of four such Sunday performances in a six month period).

✦ If the organisation arranging the

performance has been granted an exemption by the Secretary of State for Education or by an LAED.

## 3. General notes

Some companies may pay the parent a nominal allowance to cover travel and meal expenses. Transport to and from rehearsals may have to be provided by the theatre company. A licensed manager or chaperone must be in attendance at all times. If there are more than 12 children involved, two managers or chaperones will be required. Groups of male and female children will necessitate two chaperones. The 'employing' company or theatre must be able to provide suitable conditions for the children such as refreshments, separate male and female washing and toilet facilities and separate dressing-rooms.

## 4. Working abroad

If a child or young person is to travel out of the country in a UK touring production, a licence must be obtained from the Chief Metropolitan Magistrate at Bow Street, London. Allow plenty of time for this application and discuss it with the relevant LAEDs.

If you have been invited to work abroad, and your production requires the participation of children from that country, get authoritative advice about local regulations, and try to liaise with an informed local supervisor or manager.

*See also:*

**Health and safety** (page 156)

**Working as a choreographer with schools and youth organisations** (page 85)

**Working as a choreographer:**
Casting (page 39)

**Assistants, notators and staff producers:**
Rehearsal assistants (With children in theatre and education) (page 113)